ARIZONA PERSONAL BANKRUPTCY HANDBOOK

The Truth About Keeping Assets and Clearing Away Debts

SCOTT DAVID STEWART, ESQ.

An imprint of SDS Legal Marketing LLC USA
777 E Thomas Rd Ste 150, Phoenix AZ 85014
sdslegalmarketing.com

FIRST EDITION

ISBN 978-1-7323041-1-6

For information please write the publisher:

SDS Legal Marketing LLC
777 E Thomas Rd Ste 150
Phoenix AZ 85014

Legal Disclaimer

The general information in this book is not, nor is it intended to be, specific legal advice. You should consult an attorney for specific legal advice regarding your individual situation and circumstances.

This book is provided as a general reference work and is for informational purposes only. You are advised to check for changes to current law and to consult with a qualified attorney on any legal issue. The receipt of or use of this book does not create an attorney-client relationship with Stewart Law Group, its principals, or any of its attorneys.

Because this book was prepared for general readership without investigation into the facts of each particular case, it is not legal advice. Neither SDS Legal Marketing LLC nor Allegiant Law Group nor any of its attorneys has an attorney-client relationship with you. The thoughts and commentary about the law contained in this book are provided merely as a public service and do not constitute solicitation or legal advice.

While we endeavored to provide accurate information in this book, we cannot guarantee that the material provided herein is accurate, adequate, or complete. This general legal information is provided on an 'as is' basis. We make no warranties and disclaim liability for damages resulting from its use. Legal advice must be tailored to the specific circumstances of each case and laws are constantly changing. Therefore, nothing provided in this book should be used as a substitute for the advice of competent legal counsel.

The material in this book may be considered advertising under applicable rules.

Contents

Acknowledgments

A special thank you to my bankruptcy colleagues for sharing their legal insights and helpful ideas. To Laura Valade, JD, for her research and thoughtful contributions. And to my amazing family for their unwavering love and support.

"Courage is being scared to death,
but saddling up anyway."
— John Wayne

Introduction

Why bankruptcy? When barely treading water in a sea of unpaid bills, why not? Why use a teaspoon to bail water from a leaky boat? Personal bankruptcy is a lawful, moral way for individuals to find permanent debt relief. That is a tremendously good thing, a real life-changer. Imagine being back in control of your family's lifestyle. How powerful could that be for you and your loved ones?

As attorneys, we know how financial troubles creep into all aspects of daily life. Money problems are often the root of marital disharmony, family conflict, and career issues. The burden of carrying around an unmanageable debt-load is tremendous. Your life doesn't have to be that way.

Think about this. No more arguing with your spouse about budgeting and unpaid bills. No more stressing over debt collector calls and creditor threats to repossess your car or foreclose on your home. No more distractions while you're on the job working. Excessive debt strangles happiness. This may be hard to wrap your head around, but federal bankruptcy law offers individuals a debt cure that has both a constitutional and biblical basis.

Indebtedness (and debt collectors) can make people feel ashamed, embarrassed, humiliated, and frustrated for not being able to pay what is owed. But punishing emotions like those are misplaced. You can't pay what you can't pay! Don't sentence yourself to a self-imposed debtor's prison. There is justification – legally, ethically, and morally – in requesting judicial intervention to help manage, reduce, and eliminate liabilities.

Bankruptcy in the U.S. Constitution

The U.S. Constitution, Article I, Section 8, grants Congress authority to establish bankruptcy laws, creating the basis of a uniform national legal system specifically for bankruptcy and insolvency. Individuals can overcome barriers to financial freedom by petitioning for bankruptcy relief.

Federal law allows people living in the U.S., citizens and noncitizens, to legally request relief from uncontrollable, unpayable debts. Doing so is both lawful and ethical. There are no debtor's prisons or workhouses here! Individuals have the right to seek freedom from debt.

And in that process, to use bankruptcy proceedings to renegotiate contracts under better terms and shake off creditor lawsuits, property seizures, garnishments, foreclosures, and evictions.

Biblical Basis for Merciful Debt Forgiveness

Bankruptcy is a moral way of stopping circumstances from worsening. Of preventing debt-bondage from tightening around you and your family. Does spiraling debt help raise your kids? How does being overwhelmed all the time improve employment opportunities? Are you struggling through each day with a ton of stress on your shoulders? Life needn't be this way.

We don't have far to look for higher authority. The discharge of debts in bankruptcy has biblical origins. Reference is made to an economic fresh start for the debtor who is unable to repay obligations; and an act of mercy by the creditor who is rewarded by God. Debt forgiveness is set forth very specifically in the Old Testament, Book of Deuteronomy:

> *At the end of every seventh year, cancel all debts. This is the procedure: Everyone who has lent money to a neighbor writes it off. You must not press your neighbor or his brother for payment:*
> *All-Debts-Are-Canceled — GOD says so.*
>
> – Deuteronomy 15:1-2 MSG

On balance, the Book of Proverbs advises against taking on obligations because of the bondage of indebtedness:

> *The poor are always ruled over by the rich, so don't borrow and put yourself under their power.*
>
> – Proverbs 22:7 MSG

At law, the one who borrows money from another, by agreement, must pay it back. Speaking morally, a borrower who cannot repay the debt should be met with mercy. The creditor who forgives the debt, even in a bankruptcy setting, is blessed by God for this merciful act. Be mindful, there have been innumerable debtors before you who could not pay and as many or more creditors who forgave those contractual obligations. You can do this.

Bankruptcy Can Right Your Financial Ship

Do monthly obligations exceed your ability to pay them? That is insolvency, a serious situation. The bankruptcy process is, by analogy, your way to "right the ship." Your personal, financial, and, yes, spiritual ship.

In nautical terms, to "right the ship" is to correct an unbalanced load. Because the ship is listing, or leaning too far over to one side, it needs righting. That is, the ship needs to be rebalanced so it sits upright in the water before continuing on its course. Bankruptcy is an opportunity to right your ship. To get back on course and start navigating toward a better future.

Bankruptcy is the process of shifting heavy crates (debts) to balance the whole cargo. It's about releasing ballast so the ship can ride higher in the water. It's about identifying and choosing what cargo to throw into the deep blue sea (discharged debts) and what precious cargo (exempt assets) to keep safe in the ship's hold. Some things must be tossed overboard in order for the ship, along with captain and crew, to keep journeying to their ultimate destination. In a Chapter 7 bankruptcy, for example, the debtor may keep the older 4-door sedan that's paid for (debt-free precious cargo) and let the bank repossess the late model SUV. Farewell loan payments and high insurance premiums!

Sometimes the wisest action is to seek a do-over. It takes courage to admit you're not in control of your financial affairs, but ultimately a fresh start after bankruptcy puts you in the best position to take care of your needs and provide for your loved ones. You'll be in a better position to give to your church or favorite charity.

How often have you dreamed what life could be like "if only" there were fewer bills to pay each month? Allegiant Law Group wants to help you right your financial ship and set a new course with the wind at your sails.

Before getting into details, a few clarifications. We use "personal bankruptcy" and "consumer bankruptcy" interchangeably as both refer to individuals filing Chapter 7 or Chapter 13. The topics discussed in this handbook are intended to be an overview.

Bankruptcy law is complicated stuff and covers far more than we could possibly fit on these pages. Just so you know, we have lots more information on our website. Be sure to visit www.AllegiantLawAz.com. Read more about the subjects that interest you most, whether that's non-dischargeable debts or Chapter 7 means testing.

We're here to help.

"I love money. I love everything about it. I bought some pretty good stuff. Got me a $300 pair of socks. Got a fur sink. Let's see, bought an electric dog polisher. A gasoline-powered turtleneck sweater, and, of course, I bought some dumb stuff, too." — *Steve Martin*

1

What Is Personal Bankruptcy All About?

When is the time right to file for personal bankruptcy protection? If struggling to pay bills, month after month, then absolutely consult an experienced bankruptcy attorney to analyze your current debt situation and explain available legal options with specificity. Delay can increase the risk of lawsuits, add to your financial burden, and diminish your ability to keep assets.

Initiating bankruptcy proceedings is far better than being sued, having wages garnished, property repossessed, and home foreclosed on before seeking judicial intervention in bankruptcy court. Get out in front of the storm and stay there.

Our Bankruptcy Court and Laws

Bankruptcy is federal law and bankruptcy courts are federal courts created under Article I of the U.S. Constitution. All cases filed in Arizona are under the exclusive jurisdiction of the U.S. Bankruptcy Court, District of Arizona. (In limited circumstances, a case can be removed from Arizona to another state.) There are no state bankruptcy courts. State law does matter in a lot of ways, though, as with exempt property and definition of fraud. The controlling statute is the U.S. Bankruptcy Code. 11 USC §§ 101, et seq.

Although our focus is only on consumer bankruptcy – Chapter 7 Liquidation and Chapter 13 Adjustment of Debts of an Individual with Regular Income – there are many other chapters in the Bankruptcy Code. There are bankruptcy rules of court to follow, too. There are the Federal Rules of Bankruptcy Procedure along with local rules of court for Arizona. A case can be dismissed if court rules are not complied with.

Two different dismissals are possible. A bankruptcy case can be dismissed "without prejudice," allowing the person to refile without penalty. Typically, dismissal without prejudice results from a technical error. By contrast, the case that is dismissed "with prejudice" cannot be refiled until after the time bar is lifted. It's a penalty. That's because the debtor did something wrongful, defrauded the court, filed multiple cases, concealed assets, obstructed creditors, among other things.

Can the judge's order be appealed? Final orders and rulings by the bankruptcy judge are appealable, including a dismissal with prejudice. Appeals are heard by a district court judge in U.S. District Court. Or by a Bankruptcy Appellate Panel (BAP) made up of three bankruptcy judges. Under certain conditions, a direct appeal may be taken to the U.S. Court of Appeals (Arizona is in the Ninth Circuit), which is also the next appellate level from the district court and BAP. Although rare, the Ninth Circuit decision may be appealed to the U.S. Supreme Court.

Does It Matter How Far in Debt You Are?

Along with income, how much is owed and the kind of debt involved are important in deciding on either Chapter 7 or Chapter 13. When certain requirements are met, creditors can initiate involuntary bankruptcy proceedings against a debtor. In all other instances, the individual decides whether to file a voluntary petition for bankruptcy protection.

What Are the Main Purposes of Bankruptcy?

When a voluntary petition is properly filed with the Clerk of the U.S. Bankruptcy Court, a statutory injunction called the "automatic stay" immediately goes into effect. The automatic stay is protective, exemplifying three important purposes of bankruptcy:

1. Protect the debtor from being impoverished or sued without end;
2. Protect the bankruptcy estate from being diminished unnecessarily and unfairly; and
3. Protect creditors so that a fair and equal distribution of non-exempt assets can occur.

You'll read about Arizona's statutory exemptions in Chapter 4. For now, think of them as the safety net that protects specific assets belonging to the bankruptcy debtor. (For instance, the debtor's IRA or 401k is exempt property in personal bankruptcy.)

There are strict laws protecting people from debt collection activities before and after the bankruptcy petition has been filed. Bill collectors and creditors who violate these laws face punishment and stiff fines. The Fair Debt Collection Practices Act (FDCPA) is one such consumer protection law, one you should know more about. You can learn how the FDCPA protects consumers from abusive collection practices at www.AllegiantLawAz.com.

Reasons To File Personal Bankruptcy

Like many others looking to bankruptcy for lasting solutions, you are probably a bit uneasy about the court process. Even those who have been through bankruptcy in the past can feel intimidated. Remember, bankruptcy law is designed to help ordinary people overcome very tough financial circumstances. Why? Because being trapped in debt is no way to live. Hire a competent lawyer to guide you through the entire bankruptcy process. A lawyer who will be at your side during the mandatory Meeting of Creditors and any other hearings. You don't have to go it alone.

By now, you must be wondering what bankruptcy can do for you personally. Petitioning for relief under a consumer bankruptcy chapter – Chapter 7 or Chapter 13 – offers genuine relief from many types of debt, including:

- Medical bills;
- Automobile loans and other installment loans;
- Unpaid rents from lease agreements;
- Court judgments;
- Some vehicular accident debts;
- Utility bills;
- Credit card balances;
- Unsecured loans;
- Home mortgages;
- Balances due following home foreclosure; and
- Certain income taxes.

Additionally, filing the bankruptcy petition provides instant protection from creditors until the court sorts things out by:

- *Stopping bill collectors from contacting you.*

Are bill collectors calling you at home or at work,

emailing you, sending collection letters, or knocking on your door demanding payment?

- *Stopping creditor lawsuits against you.*

Are you already being sued on an obligation you cannot pay?

- *Stopping evictions, at least temporarily.*

Do you need more time to find a new place to live that's more affordable?

- *Stopping home foreclosures.*

Have you defaulted on your mortgage or deed of trust?

- *Stopping wage garnishments.*

Is a judgment creditor garnishing your wages, making it even more difficult for you to pay other bills?

- *Stopping repossession of vehicles or other property.*

Is a lender ready to repossess the car and bill you for costs of repossession, too?

- *Stopping collection of unpaid medical bills.*

Are some of your biggest expenses a result of emergency hospital care, surgery, and other medical treatments?

- *Stopping the shut-off of utilities.*

Are services to your home to be turned off?

What if a debt collector contacts you after bankruptcy is filed? Every creditor listed in the petition will receive notice of the bankruptcy. Any creditor or debt collector calling or contacting you directly after filing should be told of the pending bankruptcy case. Have your case info by the phone with case number, filing date, and your attorney's contact information. State that you are not to be contacted again and to direct all communications and correspondence to your attorney. If a collector ignores the warning, notify your attorney immediately. There are severe sanctions for violating the automatic stay.

With few exceptions, filing a petition with the bankruptcy court stops the craziness of trying to negotiate with each creditor independently. Bankruptcy will help you fix your entire debt picture without a single creditor gaining unfair advantage of your situation. As you'll see, fairness is a key concept in bankruptcy.

Worried What People Will Think and Say?

Will everyone know you filed for bankruptcy? Your church? Your friends, distant relatives, and neighbors? Unless you disclose information voluntarily, yes and no. Technically, anyone can look-up bankruptcy filing information as it is a matter of public record. Legal notice is also published in designated Arizona newspapers for a readership of lawyers and real estate people (for example, Tucson's Daily Territorial is Pima County government's official newspaper for public notices). Unless someone in your social circle is also a creditor, it's unlikely anyone will go through the hassle of tracking down your bankruptcy information.

What about your employer? If a writ of garnishment was served on your employer already, then the employer is also notified of the bankruptcy so the wage garnishment can be stopped. In a Chapter 13 case, the debtor's employer receives notice of bankruptcy because a payroll deduction typically implements the court-approved three- to five-year Chapter 13 payment plan.

Personal Bankruptcy Protection Under Chapter 7 and Chapter 13

Each filing chapter of the U.S. Bankruptcy Code addresses a certain category of debtor. Generally, most individuals file for personal bankruptcy relief under Chapter 7 (68%) or Chapter 13 (32%). Hence the focus of this book and Allegiant Law Group's bankruptcy practice.

Spouses may choose to file together, individually, or one may choose not to file at all. Although creditors could file an involuntary Chapter 7 petition against a debtor, that is an infrequent occurrence in consumer bankruptcy.

What Is a Bankruptcy Discharge?

To understand bankruptcy proceedings, you need to know what a bankruptcy discharge is all about. A discharge order from the bankruptcy court releases the petitioner from the legal obligation to pay discharged debts. Debtor's personal liability on discharged debts is eliminated. Creditors cannot sue post-bankruptcy to try and collect more money on a discharged debt.

Secured debts are a little different. The secured creditor that loaned money so the debtor could buy a car, for instance, has the right to repossess the collateral (the car) if the loan goes unpaid. Unless the debt is reaffirmed, the creditor will repossess the collateral as early in the case as is possible. But that's the end of it. Once the car has been collected, the auto lender cannot go after the purchaser for any unpaid balance. The debtor's personal liability gets permanently erased with the discharge.

Talk to your attorney before reaffirming any debt. Reaffirmation means the debtor and creditor agree the contract will continue post-bankruptcy. That can create a dicey situation for an individual if finances don't improve right away.

Already feeling guilty about not repaying certain obligations? Although not recommended, you could repay a discharged debt after the case is closed when the money picture improves. But there is no legal responsibility to do so. People have their reasons for doing this. To keep the peace at home, for example, when money was borrowed from the other spouse's parents. Just don't jeopardize what you've accomplished through bankruptcy.

Because personal liability on all discharged debts is forever extinguished, creditors cannot come after the individual later and try to collect more money. If they do, then they violate a federal court order (the discharge order). Tell your attorney.

A word of caution. Not all debts are dischargeable in bankruptcy. Obligations stemming from an automobile accident in which the debtor was convicted of DUI would not be dischargeable. Nor are debts involving fraud against a creditor. Domestic support obligations (DSOs) for child support, spousal maintenance, and alimony are also non-dischargeable.

Filing for bankruptcy can still provide an opportunity to manage those non-dischargeable obligations by creating a repayment plan that considers your income, expenses, and ability to pay. With that in mind, removing the debts that are dischargeable can put people in a much better position to pay the debts that are not dischargeable, such as child support.

Chapter 7 Is the Liquidation Bankruptcy

Most people are somewhat familiar with the Chapter 7 liquidation bankruptcy, called the "fresh start" bankruptcy. Liquidation involves selling the debtor's non-exempt assets, if any, with the cash proceeds used to pay creditors. When those proceeds are exhausted, any remaining creditors are left unpaid with the court's discharge order.

Regarding exempt and non-exempt assets, those filing Chapter 7 will claim Arizona's many exemptions. This will protect most, perhaps all, of their personal property and assets. Not everyone qualifies for Chapter 7, though, because eligibility depends upon results of the means test – calculations involving income and expenses.

Chapter 13 Is the Individual Debt Adjustment Bankruptcy

The Chapter 13 individual debt adjustment bankruptcy is also known as a wage earner reorganization. Chapter 13 lets debtors create a repayment plan which they and their creditors must abide by. These plans last from three to five years, depending upon the circumstances. Yes, it's a big commitment, but worth it for many people.

Each plan is tailored to the debtor's income and ability to pay. Obligations are renegotiated until the entire plan is realistically manageable for that debtor. When the plan is completed, the petitioner receives the discharge. As with other chapters, the federal court's discharge order eliminates personal liability on the remaining debt. Most individuals with significant non-exempt assets (such as a vacation home that is not a primary residence) will opt for Chapter 13.

Can You Switch Chapters Later?

After the Chapter 7 case has commenced, it may be converted to a Chapter 13. Assuming the debtor is eligible, the Chapter 13 case could be converted to Chapter 7. Also, should circumstances improve such that the petitioner no longer needs bankruptcy relief ("I won the lottery!") or has a change of heart and wants to end further proceedings, then he or she may ask the court to dismiss the case altogether.

Will Bankruptcy Impact Your Credit Score?

Most people worry about their credit scores as bankruptcy does appear on credit reports. Yes, filing for bankruptcy will have a negative impact on credit scores for a time. For 10 years the Chapter 7 bankruptcy filing and discharge will be posted by all three credit reporting bureaus – Experian, TransUnion, and Equifax – and will lower that person's credit score. (Of course, a long history of unpaid bills lowers credit scores, too, even when bankruptcy is never filed.) A Chapter 13 bankruptcy and discharge remains on one's credit report for seven years.

When a potential lender runs a credit report, the bankruptcy shows up in the borrower's credit history along with the FICO or similar credit score. A new lender may not offer the best deal, but is still likely to extend credit to the applicant.

Creditworthiness can be rehabilitated and will bounce back relatively quickly. With credit rehabilitation, the benefits of bankruptcy far exceed the detriments for most people. There are many ways to rebuild credit scores immediately after bankruptcy, something we talk about more in Chapter 9.

"He who loses money, loses much; He who loses a friend, loses much more; He who loses faith, loses all."
— Eleanor Roosevelt

2

How Do You Know Which Chapter?

Bankruptcy may be the best path forward, but which chapter is the proper one? Be mindful, we are only addressing personal bankruptcy filings under Chapter 7 (liquidation) and Chapter 13 (wage earner reorganization). There are plenty of negatives associated with out-of-control debt, something you are already experiencing. Fortunately, the personal bankruptcy process offers relief immediately so things can be sorted out once and for all.

We have tried to answer the more commonly asked questions in this book. Truth is, you will need to provide lists of debts, lawsuits, property and assets, income, and expenses to the bankruptcy attorney for review and analysis. All that information is necessary before deciding which chapter to file under and what the discharge order can cover. Ultimately, the lists and information provided will be used to complete the petition and forms filed with the Clerk of the Bankruptcy Court. Generally, Chapter 7 asset cases are more complex than non-asset cases and Chapter 13s are more complex than Chapter 7s. Because everyone's circumstances are unique, each personal bankruptcy is tailored to the specific situation.

Chapter 7's Means Test Calculation

Whenever someone seeks our help with personal bankruptcy, the attorney starts by determining if that client qualifies for Chapter 7. If not Chapter 7, then Chapter 13 is the way to go forward. How does the attorney know? By making the means test calculation – that's "means" as in earnings and financial resources.

The means test answers a threshold question in all liquidation bankruptcies. The initial pleadings must show the judge, trustee, and creditors why the petitioner cannot afford to pay his or her debts. (Bankruptcy lawyers call this overcoming the "presumption of Chapter 7 abuse.") There is no passing or failing the means test. If the numbers are there, then the Chapter 7 case may go forward. But when the numbers aren't there, the Chapter 7 should be dismissed. Dismissal is not the end of the story, though. There are alternatives, such as converting the case to a Chapter 13 or filing a new Chapter 7 petition at a later date.

Now you know that to qualify for Chapter 7 relief, the petitioner must satisfy the means test. Your bankruptcy lawyer will run the numbers before filing to determine in advance whether you satisfy the means test or not. Or whether it's a threshold case.

The means test calculation points the debtor in one of two directions:

- File Chapter 7 because this individual genuinely lacks the financial resources necessary to complete a repayment plan; or
- File Chapter 13 because this individual has the means to make payments on certain obligations under a three- to five-year repayment plan.

What if there's an emergency, like a lawsuit? For those who need to act fast, an emergency petition can be filed to stop foreclosure, creditor lawsuits, repossession, and the like. With exigent circumstances prompting the filing, it's unlikely the means test analysis has been conducted yet or that the necessary documentation has been assembled to determine whether Chapter 7 is truly appropriate for this debtor. Even with an emergency petition, the means test calculation must be done, and all schedules, financial statements, and disclosures filed in 14 days unless the court grants an extension. On that note, anyone who filed an emergency petition on their own should consult an attorney immediately, so the case does not get dismissed.

Difference Between Dischargeable and Non-Dischargeable Debts

Another concern has to do with the type of debts the petitioner is burdened with. Not every financial obligation is dischargeable in bankruptcy. On one hand, dischargeable debts are discharged, or extinguished, at the end of the case – personal liability is gone for good thanks to the judge's discharge order. That discharge order is very general, though, and does not list the discharged debts (as nice as that would be). The attorney can explain the discharge order to the client directly because what it covers will depend upon specific facts and how the case proceeded.

On the other hand, non-dischargeable debts remain at the end of the case so the debtor still has to pay them. That's because bankruptcy law is protecting a category of creditors, such as child support recipients. There are many public policy reasons for why certain debts were made non-dischargeable by federal law. Yet even among some non-dischargeable debts, such as recent unpaid income taxes, establishing "undue hardship" could change the outcome. Starting with the initial consultation, the bankruptcy lawyer begins assessing how each debt should be categorized for treatment under current law.

What Debts Are Dischargeable?

The kinds of debts that are dischargeable in Chapter 7 and Chapter 13 include everything that is not a non-dischargeable debt. Absent fraud, as discussed below, most debts will be discharged including unpaid installment loans, rents and leases, credit card bills, hospital bills and medical expenses, and much more.

What Are Non-Dischargeable Debts?

Some debts are excepted, or excluded, from discharge by federal statute. Among those are two kinds:

1. Debts that are automatically non-dischargeable.
2. Debts that are non-dischargeable only when the creditor makes a challenge and prevails at trial (called a non-dischargeability determination).

Non-dischargeable obligations can form the basis for case dismissal and give the judge cause to deny a discharge order.

Debts of the automatically non-dischargeable kind include:

- **Domestic Support Obligations**

DSOs include child support, spousal maintenance, and alimony. 11 USC § 523(a)(5,15)

- **Recent Federal, State, and Local Taxes**

This is a complex area, so rely on an experienced attorney to review your tax liability situation going back several years. Generally, taxes are priority claims for unpaid recent income taxes, property taxes, employment taxes, withholding taxes, and excise taxes. 11 USC § 523(a)(1).

- **Criminal Restitution**

For example, when the debtor was convicted of a crime and ordered to pay restitution as a term of probation, that restitution is not dischargeable in bankruptcy.

- **Driving Under the Influence**

A debtor convicted of DUI will not be able to get criminal fines discharged. 11 USC § (a)(9).

- **Government Fines and Penalties**

These include things like speeding tickets and parking violations assessed a fine or penalty.
11 USC § 523(a)(7).

- **Unscheduled Debts**

Ones not included with the petition's schedules in time for the creditor to file a proof of claim or object to a discharge of the specified debt.
11 USC § 523(a)(3).

- **Student Loans**

These include private, state, and federal loans along with obligations to repay scholarships and other benefits. The only exception is a court determination of "undue hardship." 11 USC § 523(a)(8).

There are always exceptions! Every debt must be carefully examined. When an exception to non-dischargeability applies, as with the undue hardship exception to the student loan or unpaid tax, then that becomes part of the attorney's bankruptcy strategy.

Debts that are non-dischargeable only when the creditor makes a timely challenge and wins at trial include:

- **Fraud**

  There are different ways to defraud a creditor. For example, by making materially false statements about finances in order to mislead the creditor who relied on those misrepresentations. Excessive spending or "loading up" in anticipation of bankruptcy is often fraudulent, too. 11 USC § 523(a)(2).

- **Willful, Malicious Injury**

  We are talking about damages for personal injury here. In this situation, the victim must prove at trial that the debtor willfully and maliciously caused injury to another person or other's property.
  11 USC § 523(a)(6).

By now you must be wondering about the differences between the two consumer bankruptcy chapter filings. Pros and cons of Chapter 7 and Chapter 13 are up next.

"An investment in knowledge pays the best interest."
— Benjamin Franklin

3

What To Provide Your Attorney When You Meet

The information and documentation required for Chapter 7 and Chapter 13 are essentially the same. Whether to file, which chapter to file under, whether liquidation of non-exempt assets will be required, and a host of other questions cannot be answered with certainty until the information gathering phase and disclosures have been made. The first part of the attorney's legal strategy is absolutely dependent upon the facts presented – there is no fiction in bankruptcy, just facts.

There are some pros and cons associated with the different consumer bankruptcy chapters, or orders for relief, and we'll cover some of those later. After all, the detriment Chapter 7 poses for one person could prove to be a benefit to another. Every bankruptcy depends upon the individual's unique situation, the exemptions that person claims, and the non-exempt assets he or she owns, if any. The lawyer cannot determine which chapter is right for this debtor until a legal strategy gets firmed up with the facts.

Starting the conversation with an attorney is a big step toward educating yourself about bankruptcy law as it applies to you and, secondly, toward resolving your financial problems in a reasonable fashion so you can get a fresh start. Anytime you are unsure of whether the information about an account, a particular document, or other disclosure is important, go over it with the attorney. The lawyer's job is to sort all of these details out one-by-one, apply the law, and determine if it's relevant to the case.

Everyone with Allegiant Law Group sympathizes and cares very much about helping you through your financial difficulties, but a great deal of information will be needed from you before filing the petition. With bankruptcy, filing and discovery happen simultaneously!

Should an emergency petition be needed because a creditor filed suit, for instance, there is limited time available (14 days) to file the mandatory mailing list, schedules, and disclosures. Attorney ethics require due diligence in preparing the petition, schedules, payment plan if applicable, statement of intent for secured property, statement of financial affairs, and so on. For the best possible results and a timely discharge, trust and cooperation between attorney and client are necessary from the very outset of the representation.

There is a natural tendency to want to keep private any mistakes, misjudgments, or self-inflicted problems that might have added to one's current financial situation. Many people feel guilty for things that were never in their control in the first place, such as medical expenses following a serious illness. Even when it's clearly not a matter of fault, most people resist sharing financial information with anyone other than their accountant or tax advisor. With bankruptcy, the individual must spill the beans for the bankruptcy lawyer to be effective at making the best case.

The attorney you meet is not there to judge, but to prepare a case that obtains the full extent of debt relief you are entitled to by law with the best possible outcome for you and your family. The attorney knows you would not be there in the first place, asking for legal advice, if not for unrelenting creditors and the threat of lawsuits, liens, and loss of assets. This isn't about whether you're a good person, spent money foolishly, or couldn't get a better paying job. The attorney knows you're in a bad situation, that your family is suffering, and that relief from creditors and debts is needed before anything will improve.

Given the seriousness of the challenge ahead, to best represent you in court, to present the facts of the case in the most favorable light, you must adjust your thinking and be willing to disclose everything relevant to your attorney. Get the notion of guilt and punishment out of your head, that's not how bankruptcy works in this country. You will be your own worst enemy by not being forthright with your attorney right from the start. Having said that, we have a lot of ground to cover.

The following checklist will be very helpful in preparing to meet with a bankruptcy lawyer about your situation. Discussing options with an attorney does not mean you have to make a commitment to file right away. Even if bankruptcy is not right for you at this time, get your questions answered. Use the meeting as an opportunity to learn more about the bankruptcy process and what the law requires of you. In gathering those initial documents, you'll refresh your memory and be able to clarify the issues and talk about them with greater specificity. When you have actual details fresh in your mind, the attorney can discuss your specific questions and go beyond hypothetical examples.

So let's get to it!

Document Checklist:

✓ *Provide pay stubs and other proofs of income covering the past year. Be sure to include evidence of all household income from all sources. Whether the other spouse files jointly for bankruptcy or not, his or her income must be included.*

✓ *Provide copies of all income tax returns. Include all W2s and tax schedules covering the past four years along with 1099s, and so on.*

✓ *Provide the most recent retirement account statements and the plan summary for your 401k, 403b, IRA, or pension.*

✓ *Provide all bank account statements covering the past six months.*

✓ *Provide all bills, statements, judgments, collection letters, consolidation agreements, and other proofs of indebtedness.*

✓ *Provide a copy of your recorded deed on real property that is your primary residence, vacation home, vacant land, or other real property you own or have an interest in.*

✓ *Provide a copy of the recorded mortgage or deed of trust on your real property.*

✓ *Provide loan balances on your home mortgage, home equity loan, home equity line of credit (HELOC), or deeds of trust secured by real estate.*

✓ Provide copies of titles to all motor vehicles, RVs, trailers, or motorcycles titled in Arizona and elsewhere.

✓ Provide loan balances on your vehicles along with the purchase agreements.

✓ Provide copies of any other instruments of record on property you own.

✓ Provide copies of the real property tax bill with State Equalized Value on your primary residence and all other real property you have an interest in.

✓ Provide copies of all insurance policies. Be sure to include documentation indicating the cash value for any life insurance policies you have.

✓ Provide copies of lawsuits (include pending divorce or child custody actions).

✓ Provide copies of all judgments, any garnishments of bank accounts and earnings, and wage assignments.

✓ Provide a copy of your divorce decree, decree of legal separation, or decree of annulment.

✓ Provide copies of any family court orders for child support, alimony, or spousal maintenance, whether you are the recipient or payor.

✓ Provide a list of all creditors' claims, the amount owed, and whether the claim is secured by collateral or unsecured.

✓ *Provide information on whether you were added to another's deed, account, safe deposit box, or other titled item.*

✓ *Provide details of any balance transfers made on an account, such as Visa, MasterCard, or other credit card balance.*

✓ *Provide details of gambling activities (gambling debts can be discharged in bankruptcy, too).*

Now you have a list of what the attorney will need from you to get started on your bankruptcy. If you like, skip ahead to Chapter 5 for key procedures in consumer bankruptcy and put two and two together.

Pros and Cons of Chapter 7 and Chapter 13

There are substantial differences and notable similarities between the Chapter 7 liquidation and Chapter 13 wage earner reorganization. Knowing how they parallel each other and where they diverge will help put things into perspective.

Consider an example: To the petitioner who is divorced or legally separated, it's important to know that, although divorce property settlements in Chapter 7 are not dischargeable, they could be discharged in Chapter 13. 11 USC §§ 523(a)(5,15).

Let's go over a few more pros and cons regarding the two chapter filings. The Chapter 13 option has timely benefits, but requires the debtor complete a multi-year plan before the court will order the discharge. The three-year or five-year plan offers the benefit of time without liquidating assets. Time for the individual to consider other options and time to seek and obtain better employment. Another huge benefit of Chapter 13 is that the debtor keeps both exempt property and non-exempt property. Additionally, any debts owed may be reduced to make bi-weekly or monthly payments manageable under the plan. This is huge.

What about cons with both Chapter 7 and Chapter 13? Absent exception or undue hardship, a debtor cannot discharge his or her domestic support obligations (DSO), student loans, unpaid income taxes, or criminal fines, penalties, or ordered restitution in association with DUI, specifically, along with some other convictions. Neither chapter can undo the legal consequences of a debtor's preference of one creditor over another by paying on the preferred debt before filing bankruptcy. (With debtor's preference, the bankruptcy trustee can recover the payment from the creditor.)

With personal injury awards, the debtor's obligation is non-dischargeable if the creditor prevails at trial and the harm the debtor caused was willful and malicious. When accidental and purely unintentional, the victim's personal injury award may be discharged like other creditors. What if the debtor was the injured victim? Under Chapter 7 and 13, the award is not exempt property in Arizona law and would be available to pay creditors.

Arizona does not allow debtors to elect federal exemptions, but many states do, including New Mexico, Texas, and Washington. A federal exemption allows a debtor to keep over $25,000 of the damage award, not including pain and suffering or compensation for pecuniary loss. 11 USC § 522(d)(11)(D). Talk to your lawyer.

What About Liens?

Even when the debt is discharged, the lien on the associated property is not eliminated by bankruptcy. The general rule is that liens pass through bankruptcy undiminished – the discharge order does not affect them. But all liens are not created equal.

Say, for example, the IRS slapped a tax lien on all of the debtor's personal property and real estate holdings. After debtor's Chapter 7 discharge, that tax lien is still there. On the positive side, tax liens only last as long as the statute of limitations will allow. They expire under non-bankruptcy law when the statutory period runs out.

In Chapter 13, proceedings could reduce the tax lien when debtor's equity in the property is insufficient for the amount of the lien. There's also something called a "cram down" which refers to a tax lien getting crammed down to the actual value of the collateral it's attached to.

Under Chapter 13, a voluntary lien on debtor's primary residence, such as the mortgage on property completely destroyed by fire, could be stripped away (called "lien stripping").

Under either chapter, personal liability for the debt is discharged when the borrower surrenders his or her home to the lender. The lender can foreclose on the property and take it back, but cannot go after additional payments. The debtor may continue living there until the foreclosure sale, an opportunity to save money while searching for a new place to live.

When a judicial lien interferes with an exemption, such as a judgment lien on debtor's tools of trade and equipment (think plumber, electrician, musician, artist, farmer, rancher), then that lien may be avoided. Once avoided, the lien goes away. 11 USC § 522(f).

Here's the takeaway. There are options that a lay person would simply not know about, ones that could profoundly impact the outcome of the case. Attorney representation is essential for the best possible outcome. If bankruptcy is the way, then do it right.

Although most people consider going to court a negative, erase the fear by hiring an experienced attorney with Allegiant Law Group. That's how you ensure everything is filed timely and properly. Should there be an adversary proceeding, you'll know your rights and interests will be fully protected.

"A nickel ain't worth a dime anymore."
— Yogi Berra

4

How Exemptions Protect Property from Creditors

Every individual who plans to file personal bankruptcy needs a lesson in Arizona's statutory exemptions. As you'll soon discover, the exemptions that apply to a person's property may strongly influence the decision to choose Chapter 13 over Chapter 7, and vice versa.

Exemptions are bankruptcy secrets hidden in plain sight. Every petitioner completes Schedule C, listing all property claimed as exempt from the reach of the trustee and creditors. A wise bankruptcy strategy depends in part on the exemptions that apply to the debtor's specific property. We'll go over each of Arizona's exemptions and offer-up some examples. After reading this chapter, start discussing the best course of action with a competent attorney.

Individuals filing Chapter 7 or Chapter 13 need and want to hold onto whatever property they possibly can. They want debt relief, but they also want to keep their home lives and work routines intact. The whole point of bankruptcy is to get a fresh start, to be free from crushing debt. Bankruptcy doesn't strip people of all their property, impoverishing them so creditors can be paid a few more "pennies on the dollar." The purpose of bankruptcy is to protect the debtor, protect the creditors (who are ranked, or prioritized, by type of claim), and protect the bankruptcy estate. Impoverishing petitioners is not an option, by any stretch of the imagination.

Exempt property is outside the reach of the bankruptcy trustee and creditors. In other words, exempt property remains the debtor's property. Arizona's exemptions are fairly generous to debtors when compared to some other states' laws. The creditor or bankruptcy trustee can go after non-exempt properties or, similarly, the value of exempt property that exceeds the exemption amount. (For example, the homestead exemption below.)

Here's how this process works. Personal bankruptcy necessarily involves matching the debtor's assets with Arizona's statutory exemptions, one by one. If the debtor owns more property or has property of greater value than exemptions protect, then preparing for Chapter 13 proceedings may be the best solution. When exemptions protect essentially all of debtor's property, then Chapter 7 may be the better alternative. Carefully consider the exemptions available to you. They really matter in consumer bankruptcy.

What Is Exempt Property?

For public policy reasons, exempt property is protected from process, meaning creditor attachment, execution, and forced sale of an exempt asset is not allowed. There are state exemptions and federal bankruptcy exemptions. The state exemptions vary from jurisdiction to jurisdiction while the federal bankruptcy exemptions are uniform.

Arizona residents must apply the state's statutory exemptions to their bankruptcies along with applicable non-bankruptcy federal statutes – that's the law. By contrast, a number of other states allow debtors to choose between state and federal exemptions. In this chapter, we will only discuss Arizona's exemptions and pertinent federal non-bankruptcy statutes that may apply. There might be reason to use the federal exemptions, as with a debtor's recent move to Arizona. Visit www.AllegiantLawAz.com for more information about exemptions in Arizona bankruptcy proceedings.

What Are Arizona's Exemptions?

The Arizona list of property exemptions is a bit lengthy. We'll summarize them, one at a time, with some examples of how they work. Everyone's circumstances are different, so be sure to make inquiries based on your own situation.

Understand that debtors cannot be induced by creditors to waive their rights to these statutory exemptions. Whether written, oral, or implied, attempted waivers of exemption rights are void and unenforceable. ARS § 33-1132. (We are not referring to secured creditors enforcing a security interest or pledge on exempt property, such as a home mortgage or car loan. ARS § 33-1122.)

Homestead Exemption

The homestead exemption allows homeowners (both spouses, one spouse, or a single person) to keep the residence they own up to a value of $150,000 in equity. ARS § 33-1101. This is a very big deal! The homestead exemption covers the dwelling where they reside – the house they own, a condominium, a cooperative, a mobile home on a rented lot, or mobile home on land they own. A property valuation, or real estate appraisal, will place a market value on the property and provide a basis for determining the homeowner's equity.

Consider a few examples. If the home is valued at $175,000 and the debtors own it free and clear, then $150,000 is exempt and $25,000 is non-exempt. (Non-exempt means not protected from process.)

What happens when there is a mortgage or deed of trust on the property? If the home has a value of $175,000, for example, and there is a $100,000 mortgage on it, then the debtors' equity of $75,000 is fully exempt.

One more example. Say the home is worth $250,000, but there's a deed of trust for $100,000. The debtors' equity in the property is the full exempt amount of $150,000.

In any event, if their residence is sold, then debtors are first in line to be paid the cash equivalent of their equity up to the cap of $150,000. See ARS § 33-1105.

One more point about the homestead exemption. The exemption automatically attaches to debtors' "interest in identifiable cash proceeds from the voluntary or involuntary sale of the property." And continues for 18 months after the sale date or, alternatively, the date they establish a new homestead with the proceeds, "whichever period is shorter." ARS § 33-1101(C).

This protects, for a time, those who sold their home and have the cash proceeds, but have not yet applied the money to purchase a different house, condo, co-op, or mobile home as their homestead. Depending upon the circumstances, this could be relevant before bankruptcy is filed, during proceedings, and after discharge.

Personal Property Exemptions

This next exemption group covers debtors' personal property and things, from clothes to cars and beyond. These exemptions are available to each individual. With married petitioners filing bankruptcy jointly, each spouse has the same personal property exemptions as the other. Spouses are free to combine their exemptions onto one asset, doubling up. Or they may find it more advantageous to exercise their right to exempt certain property separately. ARS § 33-1121.01.

(Spouses cannot double the homestead exemption. Other bankruptcy strategies may help homeowners with real property debt, namely when filing Chapter 13.)

These personal property exemptions do not prevent a secured creditor from repossessing the collateral, or secured property. When the car loan doesn't get paid, the lender still has the legal right to repossess that vehicle, sell it, and apply the proceeds of the sale to the debt. In Chapter 7 bankruptcy, that's typically the end of it. ARS § 33-1122.

Take each exemption and apply it to your own circumstances. Unsure whether to claim an exemption? Look over the statute and go to our website. Make a note to discuss it with your attorney.

Household Furniture, Furnishings, Appliances

The debtors' household furniture, along with furnishings, household goods, consumer electronic devices, and home appliances are exempt from process up to an aggregate fair market value of $6,000. ARS § 33-1123. Each spouse gets a $6,000 exemption or $12,000 if spouses combine this exemption.

Food, Fuel, Provisions

Petitioners may exempt a six-month supply of food, fuel, and provisions for their family. ARS § 33-1124. This requires calculating how much food, fuel, and provisions are needed to last debtors and their dependents a full six months. It adds up fast! Debtors may stock-up on the disposable items they ordinarily use at home along with food, such as canned goods, dry goods, and dehydrated food, among other things. Parents with infants need diapers and baby food, for example. Fuel includes propane for home heating and cooking.

Personal Items

The personal items exemption is a laundry list of things people routinely have. ARS § 33-1125. These items must be used for personal, family, or household purposes and not for maintaining a business. Here's the Arizona list:

1. Clothing ("wearing apparel") with a fair market value of $500. Whether work shoes or yoga pants, include them.

2. Musical instruments with an aggregate fair market value of $400. For the aggregate fair market value, add up what all the instruments would sell for. Spouses can double the amount by combining their exemptions.

3. Livestock up to $1,000 in horses, milk cows, and poultry. (This comes up more than you might think!)

4. Wedding and engagement rings with an aggregate fair market value up to $2,000. This helps keeps harmony at home and recognizes the emotional attachment people have for these rings. Spouses can double this exemption, too.

5. The personal library of books, manuals, publications, and personal documents with an aggregate fair market value of $250.

6. One watch with a fair market value of $250. If one spouse has a valuable watch, for example an heirloom worth more, the spouses may combine their exemptions toward that one watch ($500 total).

7. Named items including one typewriter, one computer, one bicycle, one sewing machine, one family bible, and one burial lot can be exempted so long as the fair market value in the aggregate does not exceed $2,000.

8. The motor vehicle exemption covers one vehicle worth up to $6,000 (spouses double for $12,000). For the debtor or a dependent with a physical disability, the exempt amount increases to $12,000 (spousal doubling for $24,000). Generally, this is because of the cost involved in modifying a vehicle to accommodate the disability.

9. Whether for the debtor or a dependent, all prostheses are exempt. The same for a wheelchair

or motorized mobility device. There is no limit on the fair market value of these items. If spouses combine exemptions for one's disability, the spouse who owns two mobility scooters could keep both.

10. All firearms are exempt up to a fair market value of $2,000.

11. Pets and domesticated animals in the home are exempt, regardless of value.

How is fair market value determined? Valuation will depend upon the item. For instance, resale shop or garage sale clothing prices could be used to place a fair market value on wearing apparel. Livestock could be valued based on auction values. The valuation should be reasonable given what the item is. For example, it would be reasonable to place a fair market value on a burial lot by comparison to what similar cemeteries charge. A diamond engagement ring may be appraised by a jeweler, a Colt-45 by a firearms dealer, a motor vehicle by a used car dealer or using Kelley Blue Book, Carfax, NADA Guides or other reputable online appraisal tool.

Money Benefits, Proceeds

This group of exemptions addresses something of great importance to debtors – their money! What happens to the cash a person has in the bank? What about proceeds of a life insurance policy? The death of a spouse could press the widow or widower into bankruptcy, making any life insurance proceeds an essential resource for moving on.

Numerous exemptions are tailored to situations wherein debtors received cash, benefits, or proceeds. Needless to say, this is money they hope to keep. They will, if it falls within an exemption. ARS § 11-1126.

Life Insurance

Up to $20,000 in life insurance proceeds that was already paid or is payable to the surviving spouse or child, or to a child of the deceased parent or legal guardian.

This exempts proceeds when the debtor is or was a beneficiary of a life insurance policy. Spouses may double the amount that is exempt, too. Tracing the proceeds may be necessary to establish that money in a bank account, for instance, is actually the insurance proceeds and not from some other source.

Child's Earnings

For debtors raising children, any of their minor child's earnings are exempt along with any proceeds of those earnings.

What the child spent the money on would also be protected, as when a teenager purchases a previously owned vehicle. However, this exemption does not cover a debt specifically contracted by debtors for their child's benefit.

Domestic Support Order

Court-ordered family support as domestic support orders (DSOs) are exempt. This exemption protects child support money debtors receive as well as spousal maintenance and alimony.

Be mindful, these payments must be court-ordered. If one parent voluntarily gives cash or writes checks to the other parent (the bankruptcy debtor) in order to cover their child's living expenses but without a court order, then the money is not protected in bankruptcy. With a pending family law case, the judge typically enters temporary orders for child support, spousal maintenance, or both. All support payments made pursuant to temporary orders should be exempt under this Arizona statute.

Employer Benefit Program

The money, proceeds, or benefits debtors received or are receiving through an employer benefit program – health, accident, or disability insurance coverage – is exempt property.

If a debtor is the insured or beneficiary of an employer's insurance policy or benefit program, then the money is protected without limit as to amount. Nor does it matter whether payment was in a lump sum, periodic, or in installments.

Claim on Exempt Property

The proceeds received from a claim on exempt property, as well as any benefits or proceeds from insurance following the damage or destruction of exempt property (fire, flood, homeowners, vehicle, and so on), are exempt.

Say, for example, that after their insured exempt property was damaged or destroyed, debtors filed an insurance claim and were compensated for their losses under the policy. Those insurance proceeds are exempt, too. The proceeds follow the exempt property, but the exempt amount is still limited by the original exemption.

Consider another example. The debtor's vehicle caught fire and was completely destroyed. The auto insurer paid $6,500 on the claim which is now in the debtor's possession. Because the motor vehicle exemption is $6,000, the additional $500 would not be exempt. That result could be changed if both spouses combine their motor vehicle exemptions to double the amount ($12,000). Or if the destroyed vehicle was for a disabled person ($12,000 exempt or doubled by spouses for $24,000).

This is precisely how the exemptions were designed to work. There's nothing secretive or sneaky about it. Carefully consider each item of property before claiming the exemptions on Schedule C, some things could fall under more than one exemption.

Cash Surrender on Life Insurance

The cash surrender value of debtor's life insurance policy is exempt when certain requirements are met. First, debtor must have had the policy for a "continuous unexpired period" of two years. Second, the beneficiary must be debtor's surviving spouse, child, parent, sibling, or any dependent family member who relies on the debtor for at least 50% support.

Importantly, creditors may avoid premiums debtors paid when those were fraudulent transfers. For example, the debtor paid the life insurance premium to purposefully reduce how much a legitimate creditor would be paid in the bankruptcy. Also see ARS § 20-1131(D).

Annuity Exemption

There is also the annuity exemption. Debtor must have owned the annuity for a continuous unexpired period of two years. And the beneficiary must be the debtor, the surviving spouse, child, parent, sibling, or dependent family member. Again, a creditor may avoid the premiums debtor paid when determined to be fraudulent transfers.

What's an annuity? Annuities combine insurance with investment toward retirement. An annuity is a contract between owner and issuer (insurance company). The annuitant is the measuring life, meaning the annuitant's passing triggers payment of the death benefit to the named beneficiary. The owner is often the annuitant.

At retirement, the owner starts receiving scheduled payments.

Damages for Wrongful Levy

Another money exemption protects debtor's claim for recoverable damages following the wrongful levy on or sale under execution of debtor's exempt personal property. This exemption also applies to a judgment recovered for damages following someone's wrongful taking of debtor's exempt personal property.

One example is the wrongful execution and sale of debtor's vehicle. Assume in this example that the debtor paid off the loan and owns the car free and clear of any lien. But the lender's records erroneously show the debt both owing and past due. The car is wrongfully repossessed and sold. Under this exemption, a judgment recovered by debtor for damages sustained in having the car wrongfully taken would be exempt. Talk to an attorney if something like this has happened.

Money on Deposit

Also exempt is a total of $300 in a single financial institution, bank, or credit union.

Most debtors are just happy to hold onto their cash, even if the amount is modest. If there are two bank accounts, one spouse may claim $300 exempt in the first account, while the other spouse claims $300 exempt in the second account. Alternatively, spouses may combine their exemptions to save $600 on deposit in a single account.

College Savings Plan

The interest in a college savings plan (a qualified tuition program per 26 USC § 529) is exempt, whether debtor is owner or beneficiary.

A word of caution. This exemption does not include any contributions to a college savings plan if made within the two years preceding debtor's bankruptcy filing. For instance, parents started a college savings plan for their minor child (the beneficiary) and continued making contributions while their child attends college. If that beneficiary files for bankruptcy, any contributions made in the previous two years fall outside the exemption.

Employment Retirement Plan

If the participant or beneficiary of either an employer-funded retirement plan (qualified ERISA plan) or a deferred compensation plan files for bankruptcy, then the retirement plan is exempt property. Understand that any contributions during the 120 days (four months) before filing bankruptcy are not exempt, but the rest of the retirement asset is outside the reach of creditors. And it doesn't matter whether the debtor is the plan participant or the beneficiary.

Think 401k. This exemption does not apply to the alternate payee under a qualified domestic relations order (QDRO) following a divorce or legal separation. Divorce can have a powerful impact on finances, so this may be something to discuss with a bankruptcy lawyer. Allegiant Law Group can help you with this, too.

Rent and Security Deposit

The debtor who rents his or her home can still claim a personal property homestead exemption. Prepaid rent and security deposit up to $2,000 are exempt. Spouses can double the exemption if they choose.

Think about this example. The studio apartment is leased on January 1 for a year at $500 rent per month, plus $500 security deposit. Everything goes really well for the first several months. The tenant pays $1,500 in rent on April 30, enough to cover the months of May, June, and July, but is then injured and can't work for several months. The third week of May marks the filing of tenant's bankruptcy petition and the landlord is notified as a creditor. May has almost passed, so May's rent would likely fall outside the exemption. But rent for June and July remains prepaid. The debtor claims $1,500 on Schedule C as prepaid rent ($1,000 for June and July) and security deposit ($500) as a personal property homestead.

One more thing. None of the personal property exemptions above will stop the other parent or child's guardian from recovering court-ordered child support or from collecting on a judgment for support arrearages.

Educators, Firefighters, Tools of Trade

Three exemptions focus on the tools and equipment debtors own for their work activities.

School Equipment

ARS § 33-1127 exempts debtors' library and any philosophical, chemical, or apparatus used to instruct students in school, college, university, or seminary.

In contrast to the personal library exemption discussed earlier, there is no limit on the fair market value of educational items.

Fire Fighting Equipment

Fire engines, hoses and buckets, hooks and ladders, firefighters' uniforms, furniture in station, and the like are exempt from process. ARS § 33-1128.

The debtor who purchased equipment and protective clothing as a volunteer firefighter can exempt those items. (There is also a public property exemption in ARS § 33-1129.)

Tools of Trade, Business, Profession

The tools and equipment used by debtors in their respective trades, businesses, or professions, are exempt up to an aggregate fair market value of $5,000. For debtors whose income is primarily from farming or animal husbandry, the exemption in equipment, animals, feed, seed, and grain is an aggregate fair market value of $2,500. If the debtor is required by law to keep arms, uniforms, or accoutrements, then those items are fully exempt, too. ARS § 33-1130.

This broad exemption includes marketing tools like websites, domain names, and intangible work product. In all cases, debtor's primary use of the item must be commercial. A motor vehicle used primarily for business, such as a work truck, falls within the exemption (not a car used merely to drive back and forth to work). Although their tools vary, entrepreneurs, small business owners, skilled tradespeople, and professionals utilize this exemption.

Consider a community bakery where spouses own two vehicles, one for personal use and one for bakery deliveries. They have the personal property motor vehicle exemption for the family car (ARS § 33-1125) and the tools of trade exemption for the delivery van (ARS § 33-1130).

Wages, Salaries, Compensation

A portion of debtors' earnings is subject to process (non-exempt) while the rest is exempt. The wages, salaries, and compensation exemption covers the lesser amount calculated under two possible alternatives:

1. Up to 25% of "disposable earnings" per week in wages, salaries, bonuses, commissions, tips, compensation – 75% is exempt; Or

2. The amount debtor's disposable weekly earnings exceed 30 times the federal minimum hourly wage. ARS § 33-1131.

Whenever there is an order for child support, spousal maintenance, or alimony, only 50% of debtor's disposable earnings are exempt from process. This exemption applies in a Chapter 7 liquidation, but not in Chapter 13!

Pensions, IRAs

Debtors' pensions and any individual retirement accounts (IRAs) they have are exempt property. Specific pension exemptions include:

- Arizona Board of Regents members. ARS § 15-1628(I).
- Police Officers Pension. ARS § 9-931.
- Fire Fighters' Relief and Pension Fund. ARS § 9-968.
- Arizona State Retirement System. ARS § 38-762.
- Public Safety Personnel Retirement System. ARS § 38-850(C).
- Arizona Rangers' Pension. ARS § 41-955.

Public Benefits

Another essential financial resource is also exempt – public benefits. Generally, the debtor's unemployment compensation benefits, workers' compensation benefits, and public assistance received are exempt from creditors.

Using Federal Exemptions Found in Non-Bankruptcy Law

We mentioned how Arizona residents utilize state exemptions along with applicable non-bankruptcy federal exemptions. (The U.S. Bankruptcy Code has its own exemptions which could apply to some debtors' filings. For instance, recent relocation from one of 20 states allowing debtors to choose between their state exemptions and federal bankruptcy exemptions.) As you'll see, federal exemptions are available to qualifying debtors under specific U.S. statutes. The first group exempts clearly identified pensions and retirement benefits.

Retirement Benefits

Debtors entitled to or already receiving federal retirement benefits and U.S. government pensions will find their assets exempt if any of these non-bankruptcy laws apply to their circumstances:

- Social Security benefits. 42 USC § 407.
- Government employees retirement. 5 USC § 8346(a).
- Armed Forces annuities. 10 USC § 1450(i).
- Foreign Service retirement. 22 USC § 4060(c).
- Special provisions for military pensions. 38 USC § 1562(c).

- Veterans' benefits through the VA. 38 USC § 3101.
- Railroad Retirement Act (RRA) benefits. 45 USC § 231m.
- Central Intelligence Agency retirement benefits.

The retired railroad worker residing in Arizona, for example, has RRA benefits that are exempt per non-bankruptcy federal statute.

Survivor Benefits

The following survivors' benefits are also exempt from process by federal law:

- Military benefits in a Survivor Benefits Plan (SBP). 10 USC § 1450(i).
- Annuities paid to survivors of members of the federal judiciary. 28 USC § 376(n).
- Surviving spouses of lighthouse service employees. 33 USC § 775.

There may be exceptions to any exemption. When unsure whether an exemption applies to specific property, it's time to consult your bankruptcy lawyer.

Death and Disability Benefits

The next group of non-bankruptcy federal laws protect death and disability benefits paid to the following individuals:

- Work-related injuries to U.S. government employees. 5 USC § 8130.
- Unpaid wages earned but not yet paid (limited garnishment). 15 USC § 1673.
- Workers under the Longshore and Harbor Workers' Compensation Act. 33 USC § 916.
- U.S. contractors' employees working outside the country under the War Hazards Compensation Act. 42 USC § 1717.

More Money, Proceeds, and Benefits

Continuing with the federal non-bankruptcy statutes, this group includes debtors' receipt of money, proceeds, and other benefits:

- Service member's savings deposits while on "permanent duty assignment" outside the country. 10 USC § 1035(d).
- Insurance benefits payable on a deceased service member's Group Life Insurance policy. 38 USC § 1970(g).
- VA benefits. 38 USC § 5301(a).
- $9,000 administration offset exemption on federal agencies on money owed debtors under the Social Security Act, Black Lung Benefits Act, or laws administered by the Railroad Retirement Board. 31 USC § 3716(c)(3)(A).

- Discretionary administrative offset exemption on some means tested programs.
  31 USC §3716(C)(3)(B).
- Railroad unemployment insurance benefits.
  45 USC § 351(e).

We're not done yet. Check out a few more exemptions that may be pertinent to your situation.

Miscellaneous Federal Exemptions

Numerous personal property exemptions limit what can be levied to pay the debtor's tax obligation. 26 USC § 6334. Another exemption provides immunity of foreign states. 28 USC § 1609. Several exemptions apply to various Indian tribes. Lastly, debts incurred by a seaman during the voyage are exempt. 46 USC § 11111.

"Formal education will make you a living;
self-education will make you a fortune."
— Jim Rohn

5

10 Key Procedures in Consumer Bankruptcy

This discussion assumes you will meet with a bankruptcy attorney to discuss your specific circumstances and everything is clear to get started with the petition. What follows are 10 essential procedures in personal bankruptcy. These steps apply to both consumer bankruptcy filings – Liquidation under Chapter 7 and Wage Earner's Plan under Chapter 13. Because there are additional proceedings associated only with Chapter 13, we will go over those in the next chapter of this book.

Bankruptcy Schedules

The process makes more sense knowing what schedules must be filed along with the petition. Bankruptcy is very consistent from state to state. Everyone uses the same official bankruptcy forms no matter where the case is filed. These are the main forms, so get familiar with them:

- *Schedule A/B:* Property includes real property (A) and personal property (B), whatever the value and wherever located.
- *Schedule C:* Property You Claim as Exempt using Arizona's exemptions and applicable non-bankruptcy federal exemptions.
- *Schedule D:* Creditors Who Have Claims Secured By Property, such as a mortgage company or automobile lender.
- *Schedule E/F:* Creditors Who Have Unsecured Claims includes priority and non-priority unsecured claims, meaning there is no collateral or security interest in debtor's property.
- *Schedule G:* Executory Contracts and Unexpired Leases includes contractual agreements and leases that are not yet completed by the parties.
- *Schedule H:* Your Codebtors, if any, get listed as sharing liability, although not necessarily equally. This could be a spouse, a partner, or other person sharing the legal obligation to pay the bill.

- *Schedule I:* Your Income details monthly income from all sources.
- *Schedule J:* Your Expenses details estimated monthly expenses.

Debtors' Bankruptcy Statements

Official bankruptcy forms known as debtors' statements are also filed with the petition:

- *Statement of Financial Affairs for Individuals Filing for Bankruptcy* gets into every aspect of the debtor's financial picture.
- *Statement of Intention for Individual Filing Under Chapter 7* regards debtor's plan to keep or surrender collateral to the secured creditor and any unexpired leases on equipment, tools, and the like.

Completing these forms accurately and as quickly as possible takes a plan of action. Start with step one.

STEP 1: Gather Documents, Account Details, Creditor Information

The Voluntary Petition for Individuals Filing for Bankruptcy (Form 101) along with the associated schedules and statements is designed to provide all the details of debtor's situation. The debtor must be as accurate as possible. This will take some time and effort, but stay on task until finished. Be thorough. You will likely be pulling from numerous sources before your attorney has everything needed to move forward. Failure to provide the required information could result in the case being dismissed with the automatic stay lifted. Once the stay is lifted, there's no keeping creditors at bay.

Credit Report

Start by requesting your credit report from one of the three credit bureaus (Experian, Equifax, TransUnion). By law, you are entitled to one free credit report every 12 months from each credit reporting agency. Additional credit reports may be ordered for a small fee.

Search and Assemble Files

Go through your personal files, home office files, tax records, and sock drawer if that's where important papers are stored. Do not leave any creditor out. Do not omit any property you own or possess. When uncertain if something is relevant to the case, discuss it briefly with your attorney who will sort it out. After all, this is what bankruptcy lawyers do every day of the week.

Start gathering papers, documents, files, and information from memory in order to do the following:

✓ *Provide Proof of Income*

Provide proof of income, such as paystubs, for the past six months to verify income. Include income from all sources, even if part-time, temporary, a gig paid in cash, or only seasonal employment.

✓ *List All Assets*

List all assets along with valuations. Assets include money in the bank, whole life insurance policies, personal property, real estate, investment accounts, retirement accounts, vehicles, livestock, furniture, clothing, and much more. Property listed on Schedule A/B are matched against the exemptions claimed on Schedule C.

✓ *List All Creditors*

List all creditors. Be sure to include everyone who is owed money (or property) along with the amount owed. These are all your debts, executory contracts, and obligations. Obtain contact info for all creditors – the credit report will help with this.

Now is a good time to discuss the different types of creditors. There are only three categories of creditors in bankruptcy. Those creditors will have claims that are unsecured, secured, or priority. An unsecured creditor's claim has no hook into any specified property owned by the debtor (example: debtor's credit card company). A secured creditor's claim does have a hook, called a security interest, into specific property held as collateral (example: mortgage company on debtor's residence or the lender on an automobile). A priority creditor's claim has special ranking under bankruptcy law (example: IRS is a priority creditor on debtor's unpaid income taxes).

Unsecured creditors are least likely to be paid, or will be paid less than other creditors. A secured creditor can collect the collateral if debtor elects to surrender it, but that same creditor is unsecured as to the balance of the debt owed beyond the collateral's value. Priority creditors are a different kettle of fish. Absent some exception, and there are many, the priority claim must be paid in full.

✓ *Provide Income Tax Returns*

Provide copies of income tax returns filed for the past two years in Chapter 7 (or past four years in Chapter 13). Include both state and federal income tax returns. If a return cannot be found, then the debtor should immediately request individual tax return transcripts directly from the IRS. Tax returns don't get filed with the court, but they are provided to the case trustee administering the bankruptcy. He or she examines those tax returns very closely and compares the tax information with disclosures debtor made on the schedules and statement of financial affairs. What if income tax returns haven't been filed in years? Provide copies of the most recently filed returns.

STEP 2: Complete Your Credit Counseling Session

Complete your Credit Counseling session with an approved agency at your earliest convenience within the 180 days (six months) preceding the petition's filing. That's plenty of time for most. This is offered for a nominal fee, but reduced fees and fee waivers are available to qualifying individuals. The session teaches budgeting and personal financial management techniques to help participants avoid debt problems in the future. Only use an approved credit counseling agency for this!

Credit counseling is mandatory and available in-person, via internet, or by telephone. The session only takes an hour or two. (Don't worry, there's no test to pass.) The Certificate of Completion is filed with the petition. If not timely filed, then the case will be dismissed without any refund of the bankruptcy filing fee.

However, there are a few narrow exceptions to the pre-filing requirement for certain debtors. First, exigent circumstances justify a 30-day extension (filing bankruptcy before credit counseling was a genuine urgency). Second, the petitioner is a service member deployed in a combat zone. Three, the petitioner is incapacitated. Four, the petitioner's disability prevents him or her from completing the counseling.

Under the exigent circumstances exception, the petitioner can complete credit counseling within 30 days after filing the petition (the judge may order a 15-day extension for good reason). The following must be true:

1. Petitioner tried to get counseling from an approved agency before filing bankruptcy, but was unable to do so during the seven-day period after making the request; And
2. There are exigent circumstances that make it necessary for the person to file the petition

immediately (the court determines what is and is not an emergency situation); And

3. Petitioner must include a certification stating the facts regarding conditions 1 and 2 above with the petition.

See 11 USC § 109(h)(3).

STEP 3: Prepare Petition, Schedules, Statements

Meet with the attorney to begin preparing the official forms, starting with the petition. The same petition form is used to file for Chapter 7 and Chapter 13. This is no simple task. Go back to the list of official schedules and statements at the beginning of this discussion and take a closer look at what needs to be filed.

The means test calculation must be completed to determine whether the case should proceed under Chapter 7 or not. If not, then Chapter 13 is available. In a nutshell, there is a rebuttable presumption that filing Chapter 7 would be an abuse of bankruptcy law. For Chapter 7 to proceed, this rebuttable presumption of abuse must be overcome, shown to be untrue with evidence of the debtor's income. The means test considers the individual's income for the six months preceding the filing date. Timing is important!

Because of the means test, not everyone is eligible for Chapter 7. The debtor has options. An individual could wait another six months and recalculate income under the means test. Or may petition for relief under

Chapter 13 – involving a court-approved reorganization repayment plan implemented over a three-year to five-year period. Liquidation (Chapter 7) and Wage Earner Reorganization (Chapter 13) are two very different animals. Rely on an experienced attorney with Allegiant Law Group to prepare the filings, especially for the Chapter 13 plan.

Do you qualify for Chapter 7? You need to know the difference between Chapter 7 and Chapter 13 bankruptcies. Rarely does a debtor have a choice. Typically, the person will either qualify for Chapter 7 or not. If not, the only other option for most will be Chapter 13. One is not better than the other. However, they are markedly different in how they proceed, how long they take to discharge, and what the legal requirements are along the way. Although a Chapter 7 bankruptcy takes less time to discharge, mistakes can result in dismissal. The one thing you do not want is to have your case dismissed and have to refile under the same chapter (7 or 13) or file under a different chapter (13).

STEP 4: File Petition with the Clerk of the Bankruptcy Court

The bankruptcy petition is filed and filing fee paid simultaneously. If unable to pay the Chapter 7 filing fee all at once, then request to make payments in installments or, alternatively, request a fee waiver that, if granted, means no amount will be due.

Where the petition is filed is determined by where the debtor lived during the previous 180 days. If the individual lived in Arizona for the past six months, then filing is appropriate in this state. (Count 180 days backwards from the proposed filing date.)

Filing the petition sets several things in motion. Commencement of the case initiates the court's order for relief, which is a nice way of saying the petitioner is subject to the control of the bankruptcy court. The order for relief is an important benchmark in the proceedings. The discharge order, if granted, will eliminate those debts that arose prior to the order for relief, but not after. The automatic stay also goes into effect the instant a petition is filed. Should the case get dismissed for failure to file required schedules, for instance, the protection provided by the automatic stay disappears.

Can any licensed Arizona attorney represent people in bankruptcy court? No. Only attorneys admitted to the bar for the U.S. District Court, District of Arizona, practice in U.S. Bankruptcy Court. Attorneys with Allegiant Law Group represent clients in every bankruptcy courthouse in Arizona. On occasion it may be necessary for the attorney to appear for the client in some pending local court proceeding to notify the court and the creditor of the pending bankruptcy (for example, a breach of contract lawsuit in Maricopa County's Superior Court). The U.S. Bankruptcy Court has exclusive jurisdiction over bankruptcy proceedings. For many debtors, the creditor's civil case to get a judgment or collect on a judgment must be dismissed.

The U.S. Bankruptcy Court has locations in Phoenix, Tucson, and Yuma where hearings and in-person filings take place. Hearings are also held in Flagstaff and Bullhead City.

What happens when the bankruptcy case is opened? A number of things occur when a petition is filed with the Clerk of the Bankruptcy Court. The petition gets a case number, a case trustee is assigned, the § 341 Meeting of Creditors is scheduled, the creditor matrix automatically sends Notice to Creditors, and the automatic stay goes into effect.

Every creditor listed in the petition gets an official notice of the pending case. That the automatic stay prevents certain actions. And that a proof of claim should be filed against the bankruptcy estate. The proof of claim includes creditor's information, amount of money claimed as owing, whether the debt is secured by collateral, along with creditor's priority over other creditors. Although there are exceptions, creditors typically have 90 days after the initial date set for the §341 Meeting of Creditors to file proofs of claim or be forever barred.

What about a Chapter 7 "no asset" case? If the case trustee determines the Chapter 7 debtor has a "no asset" case, then there's no need for non-priority or unsecured creditors to file proofs of claim. Why is that? After examining debtor's Chapter 7 petition, schedules, and statements, and after debtor's testimony at the § 341 creditor meeting, the case trustee believes there will be no money to distribute to those creditors. No asset case determinations are fairly common with most discharge orders following quickly.

One more thing. The debtor who filed voluntary bankruptcy could later request voluntary dismissal of the case. There are a number of reasons why people change their minds about bankruptcy: It's too soon. Circumstances are much better now. There's a windfall. Don't do anything rash. Consult your lawyer before seeking dismissal.

STEP 5: §341 Meeting of Creditors (Chapter 7 and Chapter 13)

The § 341 Meeting of Creditors is named for the statute that requires it – 11 USC § 341. Debtors must appear at the meeting of creditors, which takes place 21 to 50 days after the filing date (sometimes up to 60 days later). Failure to show-up on time as first scheduled, the case trustee will reschedule. Miss the § 341 meeting a second time and the trustee may dismiss the case without cause. Certainly, emergencies happen. Contact the trustee immediately about a genuine conflict, such as a family medical emergency. Contact your attorney, who will follow up with the trustee.

As mentioned, the § 341 Meeting of Creditors is scheduled when the petition is filed. Calendar the hearing date and make arrangements to be there. A group of debtors is assigned to the same time slot, at the same location, with the same case trustee. The § 341 meeting is recorded by the trustee. Creditors have the right to be present and to ask debtors specific questions relating to their debts. (The trustee will schedule a separate examination for the creditor needing more time.)

Rarely do creditors appear at the meeting. When they do appear they are likely to ask several specific questions. This is the creditor's opportunity to question the debtor while under oath, the debtor having sworn to tell the truth.

This is the typical § 341 Meeting of Creditors experience for debtors:

- The case trustee takes a roll call and swears the debtors in as a group. The entire meeting is audio-recorded.
- Case by case, the trustee calls debtors up to the front of the conference room to interview them directly. Spouses who filed jointly go up together. (There is no judge present, just the trustee, the debtors scheduled for that time slot, their attorneys, and any creditors.)
- Debtor's identity must be confirmed with a valid driver's license or state-issued identification card. The case trustee matches debtor's social security card with the numbers on the petition.
- When the trustee requires additional documentation, that's usually discussed days before the hearing so the debtor can bring them to the meeting if at all possible.

- The trustee will verify debtor's signature on the petition. The debtor is asked whether the petition and schedules are accurate. The trustee may have specific questions about the schedules, property valuations, anticipated tax refunds, co-debtors, employment, does debtor have a personal injury claim against anyone, and the like.

- With Chapter 13, the case trustee will ask about debtor's proposed plan and its terms. Debtor's attorney will also be there to assist and communicate directly with the trustee.

- If the petition is inaccurate in some way, then the trustee can require documentation be provided or that an amended schedule be filed correcting the inaccuracy. This is all in the ordinary course.

- If the debtor moved to a new residence (which happens often), then a change of address form should be provided to the case trustee immediately.

- The trustee may declare that debtor's Chapter 7 bankruptcy is a "no asset" case. In that event, there is little more to be done other than surrender any remaining collateral to secured creditors and wait for the court's discharge order. By contrast, in an "asset" case the trustee must arrange for debtor's non-exempt property to be sold, or liquidated, so the proceeds can be applied to pay creditors. This requires additional commu-nication between the trustee and the debtor.

All of this happens very quickly. Be patient and wait for your turn. The actual meeting takes a mere 15 minutes, if that.

In our experience, clients stress way too much before the meeting of creditors. As important as it is to be there on time, the creditor's meeting is not an adversarial proceeding. No one is going to make legal arguments about why the debtor shouldn't get a discharge. The debtor's attorney is right there and may actually be the one asking the questions of a client to move things along. It's not informal, but it's not a courtroom drama either – it's an official meeting with a specific agenda.

On the one hand, if a creditor tries to argue the case or is taking up too much time, then the case trustee will put a stop to it. On the other hand, if a debtor appears to have concealed assets, failed to disclose income, seems dishonest or untruthful in answering questions, then the trustee will likely continue investigating. Be mindful, lying under oath is perjury, as is making false statements and intentionally omitting the truth. Perjury could result in denial of discharge and penalties, among other things.

STEP 6: Automatic Stay Is Lifted for Secured Creditors

Secured creditors have a security interest in the collateral securing the debt. For example, the bank that provided the car loan is a secured creditor and the car is the collateral. So long as the borrower makes the payments, he or she keeps the collateral. The debtor who decides not to reaffirm the debt must surrender the collateral back to the secured creditor. In bankruptcy proceedings, however, the secured creditor cannot just show up at the debtor's home and repossess collateral without violating the automatic stay. First, the secured creditor files a motion requesting the automatic stay be "lifted" so that this creditor can repossess this collateral. Likewise, the mortgage company cannot initiate foreclosure proceedings without violating the automatic stay. If the court grants creditor's motion to lift the stay, then the creditor can proceed. But not before.

STEP 7: Debtor Education Course

Every individual must take the post-petition Debtor Education Course before the court will enter the discharge in Chapter 7 or Chapter 13. Schedule the course sometime after the petition and schedules are filed. Be sure the course is offered by an approved agency. The course is offered online, in-person, and by phone. File the Certificate of Completion with the clerk. This is a useful course about personal financial management. Good lessons for a nominal fee. Make the most of it, there's no option.

STEP 8: Distribution to Creditors

Will unsecured creditors get any money from a Chapter 7 debtor? That depends. More often than not, the answer is "No" because it's a no-asset case. An asset case is likely to bring unsecured creditors only a few cents on the dollar.

In a Chapter 7, the trustee declares whether the debtor has an asset case or a no-asset case. It's one or the other. With an asset case, non-exempt property can be sold and proceeds distributed among creditors of varying priority. A Trustee's Sale is scheduled so targeted assets can be auctioned off or liquidated. By contrast, there is no such sale in a Chapter 13.

STEP 9: Discharge

About 90 days after the § 341 Meeting of Creditors, the Notice of Discharge goes out extinguishing the debts that preceded the petition. Your attorney can explain precisely what is and is not discharged, especially with a domestic relations order in effect. The discharge does not close the case, however.

Step 10: Closing

Another 30 days or so could go by before the court enters its Final Decree and Notice of Close of the Bankruptcy. What is closed is the main bankruptcy which has no further activity. However, adversarial proceedings could still be ongoing. We discuss adversarial proceedings in Chapter 8.

The debtor has an ongoing duty to cooperate with the trustee until the case is closed. Sometimes cases are reopened, as when property that should have been included in debtor's schedules was left out (intentionally or unintentionally). The case could be closed without a discharge, as when debtor failed to file a Certificate of Completion for the financial management course.

"Never let yesterday use up too much of today."
— Will Rogers

6

More Key Steps When Filing Chapter 13

Proceedings for Chapter 13 and Chapter 7 bankruptcy have many similarities. Both are for individuals. Both involve exempt and non-exempt property. Both require filing a voluntary petition with schedules and statement of financial affairs. Both allow for emergency petitions. Both have the automatic stay to protect debtors, creditors, and the bankruptcy estate. Both apply the Arizona property exemptions and federal non-bankruptcy exemptions. Both require a § 341 Meeting of Creditors. And both discharge debts.

However, because Chapter 13 does not involve liquidation, debtor's non-exempt property cannot be auctioned to the highest bidder at a Trustee's Sale. Instead, the Chapter 13 debtor submits a reorganization plan for court confirmation. Every Chapter 13 plan must comply with all the statutory requirements (discussed below). A good plan is reasonable and realistically likely to be completed.

Chapter 13 plans take at least three years to complete, as long as five years for cause. Only after the plan is complete will the Chapter 13 debtor obtain a discharge. A Chapter 7 discharge takes about six months or so, depending upon the circumstances. If a Chapter 7 bankruptcy is over and done in less than a year, but Chapter 13 takes three years minimum, then why doesn't everyone file Chapter 7?

Remember the means test calculation? Most people seek Chapter 13 relief because they do not qualify for Chapter 7 – they earn too much and cannot rebut the presumption of abusing the Chapter 7 process. There's more to it, though. Many individuals file Chapter 13 because they'll be better off in the end, even with three or five years of plan payments to make.

By the way, the debtor makes regularly scheduled plan payments directly to the Chapter 13 trustee, not to creditors. As with Chapter 7, the Chapter 13 trustee's role is to administer the bankruptcy from beginning to end. The Chapter 13 trustee gets paid a fee for handling the case until it's closed several years later. Trustee responsibilities include collecting debtor's scheduled payments and disbursing the money to creditors according to the court-approved plan. For the debtor, it's a bit like paying a consolidated loan. Only better.

Understand that creditors – secured or unsecured – can agree to accept less money than what is actually owed on their claims. Voluntarily reducing the amount due on a claim may be out of generosity and common decency. Or because a smaller payment from a Chapter 13 plan is better than zero payment under Chapter 7.

Why File Chapter 13?

Some people file Chapter 7 but convert the case to Chapter 13, or file Chapter 13 and convert to Chapter 7. Many choose Chapter 13 because a wage earner reorganization offers significant advantages. Namely, debtor's ability to keep exempt and non-exempt property, to keep creditors away during the entire plan period (even co-debtors on consumer debts are protected during the plan), to prevent the mortgage company from foreclosing on debtor's home, to make manageable bi-weekly or monthly payments (the trade-off for keeping non-exempt assets), and to obtain a discharge of debts at plan completion. Case closed!

Chapter 13 is for people who need protection from creditors through the bankruptcy order for relief. Matching their circumstances against the requirements of Chapter 7, they either have an asset case and face a Trustee's Sale or they simply don't qualify for liquidation bankruptcy after the means test calculation. Although Chapter 13 is sometimes a choice, more often it's the only option. That's especially true of high earners, although every person's situation is different.

Chapter 13 is uniquely suited to individual debtors who are sole proprietors of businesses or self-employed, such as an independent contractor. Corporations cannot seek relief under Chapter 13. An important requirement of Chapter 13 is that the debtor's unsecured debts cannot exceed a threshold amount. The dollar amounts in effect are adjusted periodically and, as of 2019, the current maximum allowable unsecured debt for a Chapter 13 debtor is $419,275 and secured debt is $1,257,850. 11 USC § 109(e).

(What if debtor has too much debt, secured or unsecured? Although beyond the scope of this book, Chapter 11 may be an alternative. Also, some individual business owners with substantial property may choose between Chapter 11 or Chapter 13. Talk to a lawyer about these kinds of circumstances.)

Which Is It? Three Years or Five Years?

How does the debtor know if the plan will take three years or five? It depends upon current income. How many years the plan takes to complete – the applicable commitment period – is determined by debtor's monthly income. Here's the rule:

- *3-Year Plan:* Debtor's current monthly income falls below the state median income for a same-size family. (A debtor who qualifies for a 3-year plan may choose a 5-year plan and pay less per installment.)

- *5-Year Plan:* Debtor's current monthly income exceeds the state median income for a same-sized family.

Having said that, by paying unsecured debts in full, the debtor's applicable commitment period can be shortened. A three-year commitment period is 36 months, but the plan could be shortened to, say, 30 months or 32 months. A five-year commitment period could be shortened from 60 months to 56, 52, or 48 months depending upon how long it takes to pay off all that is owed to unsecured creditors.

The debtor's personal liability to pay unsecured creditors is discharged upon completion of the plan. Think about this for a moment. The debtor can finish the plan in less than three years, yes. But if the debtor stayed with the three-year commitment period, then unsecured creditors won't receive the full amount owed. They receive a portion during the plan with any outstanding balance erased with debtor's discharge.

Plan to Reorganize Debts Under Chapter 13

Some additional forms are required with Chapter 13, including a Statement of Your Currently Monthly Income and Calculation of Commitment Period (Form 122C-I) and the Declaration of Evidence of Employers' Payments on wages received 60 days before filing the petition. And of course, the Chapter 13 Plan (Form 113).

The debtor, with assistance of counsel, has the responsibility of preparing and submitting this key plan to the court. The proposed Chapter 13 plan is filed with the petition (if the court grants an extension, then within 14 days after filing). Soon after the § 341 Meeting of Creditors, the judge conducts a confirmation hearing on the proposed plan. The debtor, along with counsel, the trustee, and interested creditors all attend the confirmation hearing.

Best Interests of Creditors Test

Here's the basic test. Before the court will confirm a plan, the debtor has to show that the Chapter 13 plan is in the best interests of unsecured creditors. 11 USC § 1325(a)(4). Why? Because they receive more under a Chapter 13 plan than they would from Chapter 7 Liquidation with debtor claiming property exemptions. To prove this, the debtor offers up an hypothetical Chapter 7 bankruptcy and compares what unsecured creditors would receive in liquidation with what they would receive under the Chapter 13 plan. When unsecured creditors are better off under debtor's Chapter 13 plan than they would be under Chapter 7 and there is no objection, the court will confirm the plan.

Chapter 13 Plan Met with Objection

What if the trustee or a creditor does object? In that event, the debtor is left with two alternatives. Either the Chapter 13 plan must pay all unsecured creditors in full. Or all of debtor's "projected disposable income" must be used to pay the unsecured creditors over the plan commitment period of three to five years, but those claims will not be paid in full. Only when the plan includes one of these options will the court confirm it.

Completing the Chapter 13 Plan

What goes into the Chapter 13 Plan of Reorganization? Here are the highlights:

✓ *Amount of regular payments.*

✓ *Duration of the plan (this "commitment period" is three to five years, but the debtor could pay all claims early).*

✓ *Total amount of estimated regular bi-weekly or monthly payments to the trustee.*

✓ *How plan payments will be made to the trustee.*

✓ *What the debtor will do with income tax refunds.*

✓ *Will the debtor make additional payments using other resources.*

✓ *How secured creditors' claims will be treated and restructured.*

✓ *Will the debtor surrender collateral to a secured creditor.*

✓ *Will the plan cure a default and reinstate original loan terms.*

✓ *How the trustee's fees will be paid.*

✓ *How priority creditors' claims will be treated.*

✓ *How attorney's fees will be paid.*

✓ *How domestic support obligations (DSOs) will be made if not paid in full.*

✓ *How non-priority unsecured claims will be treated.*

✓ *Whether default on a non-priority unsecured claim will be cured and the contract continued after the plan is complete.*

✓ *Those executory contracts that the debtor is assuming (will continue after discharge) or rejecting.*

✓ *Unexpired leases debtor is assuming or rejecting.*

✓ *Whether property in the bankruptcy estate vests in the debtor upon plan confirmation, entry of discharge, or some other event.*

✓ *Special provisions unique to the debtor's circumstances.*

Again, the debtor's reorganization plan must be confirmed by the court before implementing. 11 USC § 1325. Although a creditor has the right to object to the plan, that seldom happens to debtors represented by counsel. Still, an objection is always a possibility, one that requires additional proceedings to modify the plan before confirmation. Once confirmed, the debtor and creditors are bound by it.

The reorganization plan must be grounded in reality, no pie-in-the-sky promises without basis in fact. First of all, the debtor must be able to make the plan payments. The plan must be filed in good faith. The debtor must file all post-petition tax returns that are due. The debtor must pay all amounts required under a DSO and which first become payable post-petition. 11 USC § 1325(a).

When Do Payments Start Under the Plan?

Payments start right away in Chapter 13. The debtor makes the first plan payment within 30 days after filing, even when the plan hasn't been confirmed yet. The bankruptcy judge may grant a request for additional time, but it won't be much more time. Before filing, the debtor needs to set aside enough money to cover the first payment (whether monthly or bi-weekly) and make arrangements to continue plan payments for the entire plan period. For instance, by arranging for wage assignment to the trustee.

Wonders of Chapter 13 Lien Stripping

Lien stripping is an important tool for individuals filing Chapter 13. In debt restructuring, an under-secured creditor's claim may be stripped-down, or reduced, to match the fair market value. (An under-secured creditor is owed more than the collateral is worth.) The debtor keeps the property while paying less than the original loan amount! When the fair market value of collateral is less than the claim, then lien stripping can be made part of the plan.

What about the home mortgage? Any bankruptcy petitioner whose home is secured by mortgage or deed of trust has concerns about foreclosure, and rightly so. One of the benefits of Chapter 13 is keeping non-exempt property, including equity above the $150,000 homestead exemption. Can anything be done when the mortgage company's claim is greater than the home's fair market? Wage earner reorganizations can do a lot of things for debtors, but Chapter 13 won't permit restructuring the loan on debtor's principal residence. 11 USC § 1322(b)(2).

This is the statutory definition:

> *(13A) The term "debtor's principal residence" –*
>
> *(A) means a residential structure if used as the principal residence by the debtor, including incidental property, without regard to whether that structure is attached to real property; and*
>
> *(B) includes an individual condominium or cooperative unit, a mobile or manufactured home, or trailer if used as the principal residence by the debtor.*
>
> 11 USC § 101(13A).

Consider an example: Debtor's Phoenix home was appraised at $350,000, but $375,000 is owed on a 30-year mortgage secured only by that residential real property. The creditor is under-secured and the debtor is "underwater." Because the debtor has no equity to protect, Arizona's homestead exemption affords no benefit even though claimed on Schedule C.

Here's the basic rule. When it's the debtor's principal residence, Chapter 13 prohibits lien stripping the loan secured only by that real estate. The plan cannot strip down the under-secured creditor's claim by $25,000 (the difference between claim amount and property's fair market value), change the interest rate, or shorten duration of the loan. The Chapter 13 plan cannot "strip" a mortgage lien down to the fair market value of the property if, and only if, debtor's principal residence is the sole security for the debt. But there's more to it.

Lien stripping could still apply to the debtor's principal residence. By way of example only, a lien can be stripped down when the mortgage is secured by the debtor's primary residence plus something else, such as non-adjacent vacant land. The plan may strip a junior lien (a second or third mortgage) on debtor's principal residence, as well any HELOC (Home Equity Line of Credit). Lien stripping would be permitted on a Lake Havasu vacation home so long as it's not the principal residence.

The law regarding lien stripping is complex with ample exceptions. Attorneys with Allegiant Law Group approach the client's situation carefully, arriving at the most advantageous Chapter 13 strategies.

Will Bankruptcy Stop Home Foreclosure?

As first discussed in Chapter 1, the automatic stay goes into effect when the bankruptcy petition is filed. The stay prohibits creditors from initiating or continuing foreclosure proceedings without first obtaining the bankruptcy court's permission (granting the motion to lift the stay). Filing for bankruptcy relief temporarily stops the home foreclosure process, but for how long?

Take a look at three possible foreclosure events – pay attention to the timing. While protected by the automatic stay, the debtor pays all past-due amounts, taking a reasonable period of time to cure the default and bring the account current. If the debtor does not cure the default, then the court will lift the stay, allowing the secured creditor to foreclose and auction the property.

What if the debtor defaults during the plan, unable to make the mortgage payments? The mortgage company can proceed with foreclosure after obtaining the court's permission and order to lift the stay.

Does the debtor have a bankruptcy option if the home was foreclosed and sold before filing? Unfortunately, Chapter 13 will not help a debtor get the foreclosed property back. 11 USC § 1322(c). As soon as you have trouble making house payments, consult a bankruptcy lawyer.

What About Student Loans?

Many people are burdened with unmanageable student loans. The statistics are truly daunting. Even retirees in their 70s are saddled with student loans. Here are a few highlights from Experian's report on the 2017 State of Student Loan Debt:

- 13.4% of consumers have a student loan.
- Average number of student loans is 3.7 per borrower.
- Average total student loan balance is $34,144.
- Average student loan balance per loan is $14,872.
- 23% of consumers are in deferment on all student loans.
- 66% of consumers are currently repaying all student loans.
- 11% of consumers have student loans in deferment and in repayment.

(More student loan statistics are available at www.chamberofcommerce.org.)

Generally, student loans are not dischargeable in bankruptcy – not in Chapter 7, not in Chapter 13. Nor does it matter whether the student loan is a federal government loan or private loan. There is one important exception.

When circumstances require, the petitioner may file an adversary proceeding claiming undue hardship to the debtor or debtor's dependents will result if student loan relief is not granted. (See Chapter 8 for adversary proceedings.) The parties, or adversaries, in this court proceeding are the debtor and the student loan creditor.

The debtor has the burden of proving undue hardship to the court. Should the court determine an undue hardship on debtor or debtor's dependents will result if student loan obligations continue unabated, then the judge will order relief. Be mindful, both parties must comply with the court's order or risk being held in contempt.

How does the court determine whether the petitioner will suffer undue hardship if required to repay the student loan in full under the original terms? The answer depends upon the outcome of the three-part undue hardship test:

> (1) [T]hat the debtor cannot maintain, based on current income and expenses, a 'minimal' standard of living for herself and her dependents if forced to repay the loans; (2) that additional circumstances exist indicating that this state of affairs is likely to persist for a significant portion of the repayment period of the student loans; and (3) that the debtor has made good faith efforts to repay the loans.
>
> *Brunner v. NY State Higher Educ. Serv. Corp.*, 831 F2d 395 (2d Cir. 1987).

When the court finds undue hardship, what student loan relief might be ordered? There are several possibilities:

- First, the judge could fully discharge the student loan debt. Gone!
- Second, the judge could discharge a portion of the student loan debt, but not all of it. The same loan terms apply to a reduced principal amount.
- Third, the judge could modify student loan terms (cut the interest rate, for example).

Can you prove undue hardship? That depends upon your specific situation. An attorney with Allegiant Law Group can advise you on the likelihood of your student loan being wholly or partly discharged or modified.

How Does the Plan Provide for DSOs?

The petitioner may be under a court order to pay child support or spousal support, each of which is a domestic support obligation (DSO). 11 USC § 101(14)(A). In bankruptcy law, the DSO is a priority unsecured claim that arises before, on, or after the order for relief (the bankruptcy filing date). Support orders arise in custody cases, by decree of divorce or legal separation, or by property settlement agreement. The DSO creditor may be a former spouse, the other parent, a legal guardian, a responsible relative, or a governmental agency (for example, the Division of Child Support Services, Arizona Department of Economic Security).

Generally, the Chapter 13 plan pays priority unsecured claims in full. 11 USC § 507(a)(1). An exception, and there are always exceptions, is the DSO assigned to a governmental unit. In that instance, the Chapter 13 plan need not pay the DSO priority claim in full if the debtor contributes all of his or her disposable income to a five-year plan. 11 USC § 1322(a).

Consult an attorney regarding any child support, alimony, or spousal maintenance orders that have you making scheduled payments, even if you are current on those obligations. With a good legal strategy, there may be some flexibility with DSO treatment in Chapter 13. Just so you know, the law treats the priority DSO claim differently than it does support arrearages along with accrued interest on the past due amount. To learn more about DSO treatment in bankruptcy, visit www.AllegiantLawAZ.com.

What Happens if the Debtor Misses a Chapter 13 Plan Payment?

Skipping plan payments is certainly not advisable, but sometimes things just don't go well. What if a Chapter 13 debtor becomes unemployed or underemployed during the plan period? A medical event, job loss, plant closure, or some other economic upset can throw everything off. Debtor's monthly expenses may have gone through the roof after a family emergency. Life happens. Given the plan commitment period is 36 to 60 months long, a substantial change in circumstances is always possible.

Skipped one payment? That's fixable. Discuss with the trustee and make-up the payment. Missed several payments? Not good. The debtor could get current by making up all missed payments. Failing to timely pay under the plan as promised will get the case dismissed. Although reinstatement is possible, reversing dismissal is not guaranteed. Quick legal action and catching-up on all missed payments is needed to reinstate the Chapter 13 case.

Rather than default on the plan, debtor may file a motion for moratorium. If there is good reason and the trustee does not object, then the court can grant a moratorium, suspending the debtor's duty to pay. The moratorium is temporary, between three to six months. Still, the plan moratorium gives the debtor some breathing room. A break from the payment schedule to rally finances.

The moratorium is a brief recovery period, not a cure. The debtor will have to make up missed payments by increasing the amount. The moratorium doesn't extend the plan period, it just suspends the debtor's payments for a few months. Consequently, the debtor may pay more after the moratorium ends than before it began. Still, a few months off the payment schedule could be all the debtor needs to get back on track with payments, plan completion, and discharge.

Debtors are not always in a position to make up those missed payments. Sometimes it's the plan that needs to be changed, as when debtor finds new employment, but the new job doesn't pay as much as the old job.

Debtor, with the attorney's assistance, could request modification of the Chapter 13 reorganization plan. The trustee or an unsecured creditor could also request plan modification. For the modification to be granted, the newly proposed plan must be approved by the court like the first plan was.

Is there a last resort? When bringing the plan current is impossible. When a moratorium from payments is not enough for debtor to recover. When modification for changed circumstances is not feasible. Debtor could seek a hardship discharge or, alternatively, request case conversion to Chapter 7 Liquidation. Distressed Chapter 13 debtors should discuss specifics with counsel and take appropriate action (or their creditors will).

Living with Chapter 13

Until the case closes, the Chapter 13 trustee is a constant presence in the debtor's life. Plan payments by payroll deduction go to the trustee. The debtor needs trustee approval before incurring any new debt because owing more money and adding new creditors could jeopardize plan completion. The trustee administers the bankruptcy, beginning to end. Be aware, any non-compliance with the plan will get the trustee's attention.

What happens to the debtor who fails to file income taxes as required by law? What about the debtor who skips DSO payments in violation of a court order? The court can dismiss the case or convert it to Chapter 7 if doing so is in the best interests of creditors or the bankruptcy estate. 11 USC § 1307(c).

"Never spend your money before you have it."
— Thomas Jefferson

7

Timelines: When Can You File If You Filed Before?

The bankruptcy process is driven by deadlines, from the U.S. Bankruptcy Code to the Federal Rules of Bankruptcy Procedure and Local Rules of Bankruptcy Procedure for the District of Arizona (the local rules of court). This is very important. Counting days, calendaring due dates, satisfying legal requirements on time, these are what move the individual closer and closer to the discharge order. The date of the order for relief – the day the bankruptcy petition is filed – is the benchmark for counting backwards and forwards.

What needs calendaring? Everything! Only 14 days to file emergency schedules. Thirty days to file Chapter 7 statement of intention. Ninety-day look back for preferential treatment of creditors. Look back two years for possible fraudulent transfers (up to four years using state law). Debtor has 180 days residency in the state before filing the petition. Calendar 60 months to complete one Chapter 13 plan, but 36 months for another plan, and on and on.

Filing a bankruptcy petition too soon. Failing to pay the filing fee and not obtaining a timely waiver. Filing schedules too late. Missing disclosure deadlines. Failing to appear at the § 341 Meeting of Creditors as scheduled. Skipping deadlines and noncompliance with statutory requirements can all result in dismissal.

Allegiant Law Group uses specialized computer programming to track timelines in every client's case. Rescheduling can be done confidently. We calendar all bankruptcy deadlines and schedule each phase and proceeding. Clients are notified well in advance of all upcoming events in the case – confirmation hearings, due dates for creditors' proofs of claim, among other things.

Consider a Chapter 13 plan that takes five years to complete. That's a long time! We calendar all events through the discharge and closure almost six years ahead. When not represented by counsel, the individual has sole responsibility for keeping track of every date and proceeding. For this purpose, obtain a low-tech wall calendar or weekly/monthly planner or download a calendar app or desktop calendar, whichever works best. Do not rely on memory!

When To File If Not the First Bankruptcy

For individuals who have filed bankruptcy before, there are restrictions on how long to wait before filing a new petition. We'll point out a few exceptions, but nothing can replace specific advice from an attorney regarding a prior bankruptcy filing. To time the petition in a new consumer bankruptcy, it matters whether the previous case resulted in a discharge order or whether it was dismissed (was dismissal with or without prejudice?). Another consideration is what chapter the earlier bankruptcy was filed under. Was the previous bankruptcy a Chapter 7 Liquidation? Chapter 13 Wage Earner Reorganization? Or was the previous bankruptcy filed under a different chapter?

When was the previous case filed? If an individual files a new bankruptcy too soon after the prior case, then the court will deny a discharge. The following chart lists the waiting periods required of the individual who filed bankruptcy before.

BANKRUPTCY WAITING PERIODS		
Previous Case	**New Case**	**Waiting Period** **Start counting from the date the previous case was filed.*
Debtor received a discharge in a previous Chapter 7 or Chapter 11 (business reorganization).	Chapter 7	8 years. 11 USC § 727(a)(8)
Debtor received a discharge in a previous Chapter 13 or Chapter 12 (plan for family farmers and family fishermen).	Chapter 7	6 years. 11 USC § 727(a)(9) Exception: Debtor paid all allowed unsecured claims in the previous case in full. Or debtor acted in good faith with best efforts in paying 70% or more of the total of allowed unsecured claims.
Debtor received a discharge in a previous Chapter 7, Chapter 11, or Chapter 12.	Chapter 13	4 years. 11 USC § 1328(f)(1)
Debtor received a discharge in a previous Chapter 13.	Chapter 13	2 years. 11 USC § 1328(f)(2)
Chapter 7, Chapter 13, or Chapter 12 case was dismissed without discharge because of the individual debtor's wrongful acts. Three possibilities: (1) Case was dismissed following debtor's willful failure to comply with the court's orders. (2) Case was dismissed following debtor's failure to appear before the court in the proper prosecution of the bankruptcy case. (3) Case was dismissed on debtor's voluntary request following a creditor's lift stay motion. The Code provision against repeat bankruptcy filings.	Chapter 7 or Chapter 13	180 days from dismissal. 11 USC § 109(g) There could be an exception, even if the creditor's motion to lift stay was granted in the previous case. In California, the BAP 9th Circuit Court of Appeals denied dismissal of debtor's new Chapter 13 case because dismissal would "have produced an illogical and unjust result..." *In re Luna*, 122 BR 575 (BAP 9th Cir Cal 1991).

Revocation of Discharge

What happens if the debtor deliberately misled the court, lied to the trustee, and deceived creditors? Within a year of the Chapter 7 discharge, if the trustee or creditor discovers the debtor acted wrongfully in the case (committed fraud, concealed assets, refused to obey court orders, or some other wrongful act), then the court can revoke the discharge. 11 USC § 727(d-e). The Chapter 13 debtor's fraud will result in revocation of the discharge or, if discovered earlier, revocation of the plan confirmation order.

The revoked discharge order or revoked confirmation order certainly puts debtor in a dicey financial situation with creditors. But that could be the tip of the iceberg if, for example, the debtor knowingly concealed property of the bankruptcy estate to purposefully defraud creditors. Bankruptcy crimes are punishable by up to five years imprisonment and up to $250,000 in fines. See 18 USC § 152.

Case Conversions for Chapter 13 and Chapter 7

Nobody files bankruptcy because life and work are going great. People file because they cannot cope with their current economic circumstances, it's just too much to deal with and beyond their control. Once in bankruptcy, complicated debtor-creditor relationships can take a little time to untangle. Yes, the automatic stay stops debt collectors, but a persons' situation could change positively or negatively while the case is pending. An experienced bankruptcy attorney, the trustee, and the judge understand this, as do the creditors. Keeping the attorney informed is essential for the best outcome. Debtor's responsibilities include communicating pertinent details whenever something causes income or expenses to fluctuate too much.

What does not take the debtor out of bankruptcy entirely with dismissal could cause a switch from Chapter 7 to Chapter 13, or the reverse. For example, the debtor had been employed with the company for two years prior to filing Chapter 13 only to receive a pink-slip notice of lay-off just after plan confirmation. Unless the individual hires on with another company right away, unemployment can derail the best plan.

Conversion in marginal cases is not uncommon either. A single event or domino of bad news is reason to consult the attorney and review strategy. The request for relief may need changing with new or worsening circumstances. That's especially true when an individual only narrowly qualifies for Chapter 7 after means testing or can barely get by month-to-month after making each payment on the Chapter 13 plan.

Any debtor may ask to convert a pending case to a different chapter. Why do so? Because circumstances have improved, worsened, or changed since filing. If finances substantially improve or there's a change of heart, then the Chapter 7 debtor may request conversion to Chapter 13 at any time and keep both exempt and non-exempt property. 11 USC § 706(a). That decision must be voluntary! No debtor can be ordered into Chapter 13 without consent.

Sometimes the person's finances do not improve sufficiently to justify continuing a three-year or five-year wage earner plan. The Chapter 13 debtor may voluntarily request either conversion to Chapter 7 or dismissal of Chapter 13 "at any time." 11 USC § 1307(a). Although Chapter 13 conversion to Chapter 7 could be voluntary or involuntary, the debtor must qualify for Chapter 7 after means testing – only then will the court order case conversion. It's even possible to convert a case more than once. A voluntary conversion of Chapter 7 to Chapter 13 could be involuntarily converted back to Chapter 7! Don't let bankruptcy drive you crazy, consult an experienced attorney with Allegiant Law Group.

Get it done right.

"I have not failed.
I've just found 10,000 ways that won't work."
— Thomas A. Edison

8

What Are Adversary Proceedings?

Some personal bankruptcies will have a kind of mini-lawsuit within the main case. Separately filed civil lawsuits within the main bankruptcy are known as adversary proceedings and are between the debtor and a creditor or trustee. The debtor, the trustee, or a creditor may initiate the adversary proceeding. The parties seek a final determination from the bankruptcy judge.

There could be more than one adversary proceeding in a given bankruptcy, reason enough to hire a bankruptcy lawyer. Adversary proceedings involve litigation in court

– meaning there will be pleadings, hearings, and a trial if the parties are unable to reach a settlement. Specific rules of court apply in adversary proceedings while other laws apply to the substantive issues raised by the complaint.

If the debtor initiated the adversary proceeding by filing a complaint with allegations, then he or she is the plaintiff. When a creditor, as plaintiff, files the complaint, then the debtor (as defendant) offers a defense to the allegations raised in the compliant. Adversary proceedings are an important reason why hiring an attorney from the beginning is best.

Why are adversary proceedings even necessary? Adversary proceedings in Chapter 7 and Chapter 13 cases are filed for a number of reasons. Does a creditor object to a discharge or want to recover property from the debtor? Under the rules, a party must file an adversary proceeding in order to request the following kinds of relief:

- Recovering money or property.
- Determining the validity, priority, or extent of a lien or other interest in property.
- Obtaining court approval for the sale of both the interest of the estate and of a co-owner of the property.
- Objecting to the discharge or to revoke a discharge.

- Revoking the court's order of confirmation of a Chapter 13 plan.
- Determining whether a specific debt is or should be dischargeable.
- Getting an injunction or some other equitable relief from the court.
- Subordinating, or ranking as inferior, any allowed claim or interest to another's claim or interest.
- Obtaining a declaratory judgment from the court regarding any of these matters.
- Determining a claim or cause of action that was removed to another district court.

See Federal Rules of Bankruptcy Procedure Rule 7001.

Although adversary proceedings are always possible, most individuals will not be involved in one. Here are a few examples of why adversary proceedings are brought in Chapter 7 and Chapter 13 cases:

- The trustee can object to discharge on various grounds, such as debtor fraud or unfair treatment in the repayment of creditors. For instance, the trustee can initiate adversary proceedings on the basis of debtor's fraudulent transfer or preferential transfer.
- The Chapter 7 trustee can initiate an adversary proceeding to sever a co-owner's interest in debtor's non-exempt property when the trustee

will be selling that property at auction to distribute the proceeds of the sale to creditors.

- Debtor allegedly made a preferential transfer within 90 days of filing bankruptcy by paying a creditor, for example, who was a family member. 11 USC § 547.
- Debtor claims undue hardship in order to have a student loan discharged or modified.
- Debtor seeks discharge of a non-dischargeable debt, such as past due income taxes or domestic support obligations.
- Debtor allegedly made a fraudulent transfer. For example, the individual sold property to an employer with the intent and purpose of having the employer transfer that property back to the debtor after the bankruptcy case is closed.
- Debtor allegedly incurred a debt within 90 days of commencement of the case, presumably in anticipation of bankruptcy.
- Debtor allegedly made a cash advance of more than $1,000 within the 70 days preceding filing, presumed to defraud the creditor because the debtor never intended to pay it back.
- Debtor allegedly purchased luxury goods for more than $725 using a credit card and did so within 90 days before filing bankruptcy, a presumed fraud against the creditor.

- A Chapter 13 debtor may file an adversary proceeding to strip a junior lien or home equity line of credit off the primary residence when all other legal requirements are met. (As when the debtor is underwater on the first mortgage, leaving the second mortgage unsecured.)
- Debtor can initiate an adversary proceeding and seek damages against a creditor that violated the automatic stay.

Of course, the debtor has the right to defend against allegations of fraud brought by a creditor or alleged unfairness to creditors brought by the trustee. Because the law presumes a large cash advance given to the debtor only two months before filing bankruptcy was fraudulent does not make it so. The debtor's attorney presents evidence, including debtor's testimony, to overcome the presumption of fraud. This shifts the burden of proving fraud onto the creditor or trustee. Although it can increase legal costs and expenses, the debtor could have one attorney for the bankruptcy and another attorney for the adversary proceeding.

Did you transfer an asset inadvertently before filing bankruptcy? Tell your attorney what you did and why. The trustee could undo the transaction and recover that property for the estate.

A quick note before leaving this discussion. Fraudulent transfers can take many forms. Gifting assets before filing to keep property out of the bankruptcy estate or away from creditors. Selling assets below market value in the days or weeks preceding bankruptcy to qualify for Chapter 7. The sooner you involve a bankruptcy lawyer, the sooner you'll get the legal advice you need to avoid delays and adversary proceedings.

"The quickest way to double your money is to fold it in half and put it in your back pocket."

— Will Rogers

9

Rebuilding Your Credit Score

The decision to file bankruptcy includes thinking beyond the proceedings. What will life be like after the discharge? Imagine life after bankruptcy. How long will it take to qualify for a new home loan? When will a car loan be possible? For a fresh start after bankruptcy to really take hold, begin by staying out of debt and rebuilding personal credit scores.

When to start re-establishing credit? As soon as the bankruptcy case is closed! Start by taking advantage of manageable credit-building offers from banks and lenders. Proceed cautiously. Implement techniques learned from the personal financial management course in the bankruptcy.

Sophisticated creditors know full well there can be no new bankruptcy filings anytime soon (see Chapter 7 for bankruptcy timelines). This makes some lenders more willing to extend credit to the person who recently exited bankruptcy. So long as the extension of credit is manageable, begin by taking small steps with minimal amounts to re-establish creditworthiness. Take on only what can be easily repaid on time as scheduled.

6 Ways to Start Rebuilding Credit Scores

Improving one's credit score, or FICO score, after bankruptcy is not difficult, but it does take discipline, persistence, and the passage of time. Do not take any unnecessary financial risks. Instead, start building a solid foundation.

Examine Your Credit Report

Contact all three credit reporting bureaus (Equifax, Experian, TransUnion) and order your post-bankruptcy credit report. Examine the reports carefully. Make sure the bankruptcy is noted on every discharged debt. Errors and omissions are easy to correct by notifying the credit reporting bureau about the problem or disputed information.

Create a Budget

Create a budget and live within it, even if that means tightening your belt and giving up some non-essentials. The objectives are to pay bills as they become due and start saving a little money with every paycheck.

A budget includes all the money coming into the household and all the money going out of it:

- Income from all sources. Be sure to add in child support and spousal maintenance received.
- All living expenses. List all monthly bills along with obligations to pay support for a child or former spouse.
- Include payments on debts that were not discharged in the bankruptcy. (If unsure, then discuss the discharge with your attorney.)

Write up your budget. Pencil on paper works fine. Better yet, use a spreadsheet program that makes updating and adjusting your budget easier, such as Excel, Google Sheets, or OpenOffice. Review your budget often and stick to it!

If you have not done so already, then find ways to reduce monthly expenses. Consider cutting the cable-TV cord with free online alternatives for watching shows. Get everyone in the household on board. Don't make excuses for why you need to buy things that aren't genuinely needed.

Create an Emergency Fund

Start building cash reserves for an emergency fund. Set aside a small percentage of every paycheck and include that in your budget. Ideally, an emergency fund should have sufficient cash reserves to cover ordinary expenses for a period of three to six months. Should there be an emergency, such as a job loss or hospital emergency, use cash reserves to pay bills and maintain creditworthiness until the situation stabilizes and improves.

Pay Bills Early

As much as 35% of an individual's credit score is determined by payment history, while about 30% is based on amount owed. Make the most of credit scoring by getting into the habit of paying bills a little early so they always arrive on time.

Obtain a Secured Credit Card

Consider obtaining a secured credit card by depositing a specified amount with a bank – this is the security deposit. The credit limit on a secured credit card is equal to the amount on deposit, which could be $200 or $2,000. If the cardholder fails to pay what's due on time, then the creditor applies the deposit to the debt. Only agree to a low credit limit at first, ensuring the amount due can be paid in full each month. Use the card sparingly by making ordinary purchases for groceries, fuel, and the like.

By paying each monthly statement in full and on time, the cardholder slowly improves creditworthiness. Having established a good payment history with the lender, the security deposit is eventually refunded to the cardholder. Be a smart consumer by shopping around for the best deal with the lowest annual fee.

Obtain a Cash-Secured Loan

Another way to improve creditworthiness is to obtain a cash-secured loan from the bank or credit union. The borrower's savings account, certificate of deposit (CD), or money market account on deposit with a bank or credit union is pledged as security for the loan. The bank is more comfortable lending money after the bankruptcy because the loan is secured by money already on deposit there – the cash in the account serves as collateral for the loan. The borrower's objective is to pay off the loan on time, thereby improving credit scores. In the event of default for nonpayment, however, the lender applies the money securing the loan to the debt. Different banks offer different terms, so always shop around. And don't bite off more than you can chew.

With time and persistence, your credit score will inch upwards. There really is life after bankruptcy, and it can be a very good one. By avoiding the situations that gave rise to the financial problems of the past, and by making decisions that maximize the family budget, you can enjoy a fresh start and embrace a happier lifestyle.

About Scott David Stewart, Esq.

Author Scott David Stewart is Allegiant Law Group's founding attorney. His vision was to establish a law firm that would serve as the holistic, positive force clients rely upon in every stage of personal bankruptcy.

Scott has seen his clients and their families overcome serious emotional and financial challenges, even with the full force of personal crisis seemingly upon them. His greatest reward is in providing tailored bankruptcy solutions that help people through their struggles for positive, meaningful, often life-changing results. Lawyers with Allegiant Law Group have earned the trust and respect of clients from all backgrounds and take on the most complex and challenging cases.

Born and raised in Phoenix, Scott and his wife love the community where they are raising two daughters. Early in his professional career, Scott was Deputy County Attorney in the Major Crimes Division of the Maricopa County Attorney's Office. As a felony prosecutor, he honed his trial skills and developed the strategies for success that he continues to implement today in all aspects of his law practice. Over a decade ago, Scott founded Stewart Law Group, a divorce and family law firm with eight Valley locations.

A member of the State Bar of Arizona, Maricopa County Bar Association, and American Bar Association, Scott is AV Preeminent® attorney-rated by Martindale-Hubbell® and rated "Superb" by Avvo, Inc. Allegiant Law Group is an accredited Arizona business with the Better Business Bureau having received an A+ rating. For current news about the author, his recognitions, awards, and client testimonials, visit www.AllegiantLawAz.com today.